THE
JUDGEMENT
TRAP

Overcome the Fear of What People Think
and Unlock Your True Potential

#judgementfreecode

*Master 11 Blissful Practices to
Overcome Judgement and Be Your True Self*

SHALINI VARDHAN

notionpress
.com

INDIA · SINGAPORE · MALAYSIA

ISBN
Paperback 979-8-89588-664-9
Hardcase 979-8-89699-387-2

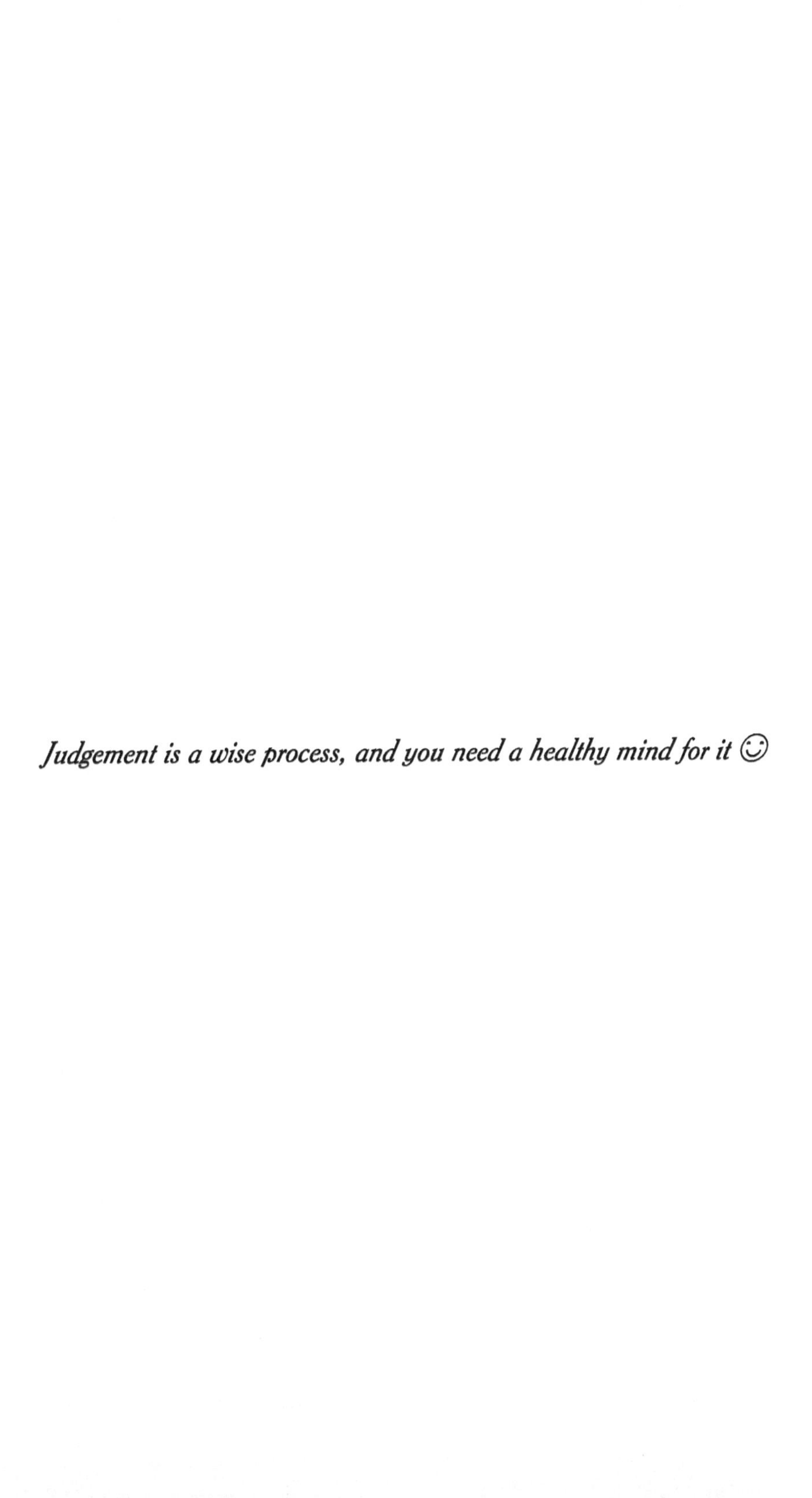

Judgement is a wise process, and you need a healthy mind for it ☺

Contents

Foreword

Fear of judgment—it's something we've all felt, right? That nagging voice that keeps you from chasing your dreams or being your true self. In *The Judgment Trap*, Shalini dives into this universal struggle with clarity, warmth, and practical advice.

Her story is as real as it gets. Growing up in a village in Nalanda, Bihar, and rising to a senior role at a Fortune Global Top 100 organization, she's no stranger to self-doubt and fear of judgment. She's lived through moments of feeling inadequate and questioning her choices. But she didn't let those fears win. Instead, she turned them into fuel for growth, resilience, and self-belief.

I know Shalini personally, and her journey is nothing short of inspiring. I've seen her struggles and incredible growth. That's why I believe in this book and its message—it's real, relatable, and packed with wisdom.

This isn't just a book of stories; it's a guidebook for navigating life when judgment feels overwhelming. Her mix of personal experiences, research-backed insights, and practical techniques make it a toolkit anyone can use.

Her honesty about battles with language barriers, cultural shifts, and that critical inner voice makes this book special. If you've ever felt like you don't measure up, her stories will hit home and remind you that transformation is possible.

She also introduces fictional characters like Mr. Bliss, representing positive voices, and others who personify internal struggles. It's a creative way to help readers see their inner dialogue and amplify supportive voices while quieting critical ones.

The Judgment Trap doesn't just tell you what's wrong; it gives you tools to fix it. From celebrating tiny wins to building your support network, the techniques in this book are easy to apply and impactful.

Whether you're a teenager feeling the pressure to fit in, a young professional navigating workplace insecurities, or someone trying to quiet the noise of judgment, this book is for you.

Reading The Judgment Trap feels like having a heart-to-heart with a wise, encouraging friend—someone who understands and believes in your ability to rise above it. By the time you finish, you'll feel ready to embrace your true self, quiet the critics, and live a life full of purpose and confidence.

This book is a gift for anyone who's ever doubted themselves. Open its pages, take the journey, and discover the incredible potential inside you.

Koustubh Kanade - Strategic Thinker & Transformational Leader from Healthcare industry, Ex B Braun, Ex Panasonic, Ex Sanofi, Ex Abbott

Acknowledgment

To my parents and in-laws, whose unwavering love, support, and belief in me have been my greatest strength. To my father, who inspired me to dream big and reach for the stars, and to all of you, who have shown me what unconditional care truly means — this book is a tribute to your endless encouragement and love.

To my husband, Kunal, whose partnership and understanding have been my rock. And to my mentors, whose guidance and wisdom have shaped my journey — thank you for believing in me...

This book draws inspiration from my own experiences and the stories of many around me — those who have successfully escaped this complex trap and those who are still struggling. It's designed to help you face your challenges quickly and effectively. Having navigated this tough path myself, I want to spare you the long, difficult journey of trial and error. My goal is to make your path smoother and more direct 😊

Why This Book is for You

Are you ready to embark on a transformative journey and finally silence the doubts that have held you back? If you're searching for a self-help guide that won't just sit on your shelf collecting dust but will reshape your life, *The Judgement Trap* is the book for you! 😊

But, let me take you on a quick tour of some relatable situations. See if any of these sound like you,

- **Public Speaking? Nope!**

  Do you avoid stepping onto that stage or into the spotlight, even though you've got something meaningful to say?

- **The "Shy" Shield**

  Do you call yourself shy just to escape interactions with strangers, wishing you were more confident?

- **Text, please!**

  Is replying to a message easier than picking up a call because the thought of live conversation makes you uneasy?

- **Party Panic!**

  Do you break out in a sweat when you realise there's a social gathering or party on the weekend?

- **Heart Racing at Hello**

  Does just being at a social event make you blush, sweat, or send your heart into overdrive?

- **Authority Anxiety**

  Ever feel nervous speaking with your boss, teacher, or someone in charge, even when you need to voice your opinion?

- **Silent Disagreements**

  Do you keep your thoughts to yourself when you disagree with someone, afraid of how they'll react if you speak up?

- **Dance? No Chance!**

  Have you avoided going to a party, worried someone might ask you to sing, dance, or do anything that puts you on the spot?

- **Easily Embarrassed?**

  Do you feel awkward or embarrassed, even around people who know you well?

- **Pre-Event Preparation Overload**

  Before a gathering, do you obsess over who you'll talk to and what you'll say, replaying every possible conversation in your head?

- **Second-Guessing Pro**

  Do you find yourself doubting your decisions or holding back from opportunities because you're afraid of judgement from others — or even yourself?

- **Big Dreams, But...**

  Are you someone with massive aspirations, but the fear of failure and criticism keeps you standing still?

- **Confident Yet Cautious (sometimes not even aware of it)**

  Are you outwardly confident—seemingly fearless in your career or social life—but deep down, still worry about what others secretly think of you? You might brush it off, but that lingering fear of judgement still holds you back in subtle ways.

If you nodded your head at any of these, The Judgement Trap is tailor-made for you. This book is your companion to help you:

- Break free from the chains of judgement.
- Stop second-guessing yourself.
- Embrace your unique voice.
- Unlock the bold, confident version of yourself that's been waiting to step out into the world.

This is more than just a book – it's the push you need to break free from your fears and live the life you've always imagined.

Preface – From Fear to Freedom

I used to think I had mastered the art of hiding – not from people physically, but from their judgement. Even back in my hometown of Jamshedpur, long before I left for college, I was an epitome of fear when it came to what people thought of me. I can still remember how deeply those judging eyes affected me. Every time I stepped out of my house, it felt like everyone was watching, scrutinising. It was as if their gaze could pierce through me, finding every flaw I was already so aware of or wasn't even there.

The stares hurt, not because of what they said, but because of what I imagined they were thinking.

I avoided drawing attention to myself in every way possible. Fancy dresses? Absolutely not. Even when my parents, with so much love, gifted me new clothes, my first thought wasn't excitement. Instead, I'd feel a sinking emotion – "What will people think if I wear this?" Their eyes would be on me, and I wasn't ready for that. I wanted to remain unnoticed, as if invisibility could protect me from being judged.

This fear didn't leave me, even when I was home. It travelled with me when, at 19, I left Jamshedpur for a completely new world in Vishakhapatnam. The cultural shock hit me hard. Andhra Pradesh was a place where everything felt different – the language, the traditions, the food, and the people. I was away from my parents for the first time, surrounded by unfamiliar faces and an unfamiliar language, Telugu, alongside English. English felt like an unscalable mountain. I could understand it, but speaking it? That was a different story altogether. Every sentence felt like a test, and failure meant judgement.

I moved into a hostel with 6 roommates who were the polar opposite of me. They were confident, stylish, fluent in English—everything I wasn't. My simple dress sense, lack of accessories, and self-consciousness stood out like a sore thumb. I was the girl who didn't know how to look "good," who didn't have fancy clothes, and who could barely keep up with conversations in a language that wasn't mine. All of this magnified the fear I had already carried for years. I was in a constant state of panic—afraid of being seen, judged, and dismissed.

My daily routine was to sit in class, always in the middle row, where I could blend in and not stand out. I feared answering questions, even when I knew the answers, because the risk of speaking up outweighed the reward. What if I got it wrong? Worse, what if I got it right but stumbled over my words? My English wasn't fluent, and I feared that my peers would think less of me if they heard me speak.

I became socially anxious, always trying to avoid interactions. On my way back from class, I would make sure to walk quickly and avoid eye contact. The idea of someone stopping to talk to me filled me with dread because I knew what would follow—questions, conversations, and the possibility of fumbling my English. The judgement felt inevitable.

But the fear of judgement peaked one day when I came back to my hostel early. I thought I'd have the room to myself, but soon after, 8 of my classmates, including my roommates, walked in. I panicked. I didn't want them to see me or ask me anything. I wasn't ready to face them. So, I did what seemed logical in my fearful mind – I hid in the washroom. Minutes passed, then hours. I stayed hidden because I was too afraid to come out, too afraid of what they would think or say if they saw me. Those couple of hours felt like an eternity, and at that moment, my fear of judgement was at its absolute peak.

Looking back, that day was one of my lowest. It was a turning point, even though I didn't realise it at the time. I was completely broken – my confidence shattered; my self-esteem non-existent. All I could see were my flaws, and I believed everyone around me saw them too. I felt trapped, not just in that washroom but in my own mind, completely wrapped in the fear of what others thought.

But something changed when the first-year results came out. I had topped the class with distinction. Everyone was surprised. But more than that, I was surprised. It was a moment of clarity, a realisation that the fear of judgement had been a prison of my own making. The truth was, no one had judged me as harshly as I had judged myself. This incident was just one story out of many and from that point on, I began to fight back against this fear. I took small steps, but each one chipped away at the walls I had built around myself.

With time, I discovered that the judgement I feared so much wasn't the defining factor of my worth. My ability, my resilience, and my character; those were the things that truly mattered. I started participating in conversations, even initiating them. I developed a sense of humour that became one of my strongest assets, and I went from hiding in the background to leading events and moderating meetings with over 100 people.

This book is the result of my journey from fear to freedom. And it's a journey you can take too.

By the time you finish reading, you will be equipped with practical techniques and strategies to break free from the fear of judgement and live the life you deserve.

You'll realise, just as I did, that you're enough, just as you are. The fear that holds you back today will become a distant memory, and you will be ready to embrace a future filled with confidence, free from the weight of what others might think.

About the Author

Born in a village in Nalanda, Bihar, and now working for a Fortune Global Top 100 company in Germany, Shalini embodies the spirit of perseverance and self-belief. With multiple management degrees from prestigious institutions like IIM Kozhikode and IIM Jammu, and years of experience navigating the corporate world, she has overcome countless obstacles—both internal and external—on her path to success.

Now living in Mumbai with her husband and two daughters, Shalini draws on their personal journey to inspire others to rise above fear, self-doubt, and judgement. She has experienced firsthand how inner critics and societal pressures can hold you back from becoming your true self.

With a passion for helping others unlock their potential, Shalini wrote ***The Judgement Trap*** to share actionable strategies, practical insights, and the lessons she's learned from a life full of challenges and triumphs.

Her mission is to empower young adults and professionals to break free from the fear of judgement, take control of their lives, and become the most authentic version of themselves.

Shalini is an aspiring author whose life purpose is to inspire others through her writing, helping readers embrace their extraordinary potential with one fearless step at a time.

Introduction

Have you ever felt lost at a party or felt a sense of fear before attending a formal get-together with unknowns? Have you ever felt anxious about attending a crowd either in a personal or professional setup with a feeling of aloofness or being avoided, with a voice within asking, "What will I do there? How will I talk to new people?" Did you ever feel hesitant before talking to the unknown with your image? Did you ever think about how people perceive you?

Have you ever experienced nervousness before presentations or on stage? Have you ever had self-doubt and thought, "Will I be able to do this, and if not, what will people think about me?"

Have you ever believed yourself that "This is my dream, but will I ever be able to achieve it?"

Are you oversensitive, a perfectionist, or suffering from social anxiety? Then, this book is for you.

And good that we met 😊

According to the National Institute of Mental Health, more than half of the world's population is suffering from social anxiety disorder, and 75% of them are in the working population[1]. This is more than just shyness; it is something to be taken care of as it affects our daily life, whether in school, university, or the office.

The reason we're connecting through this book is to show you that these challenges can be tackled. I've been through them myself and learned the hard way.

I want to help you navigate these issues more smoothly and avoid the same struggles I faced.

The book will take you on a journey first where we will decode the basic cause of this strange feeling, keeping all aspects and scenarios in mind, and then we will decode the tips, tricks, and methods to deal with the fear of judgement.

Here, you will also learn how to use judgement to your advantage and transform even the most negatively perceived judgement into a powerful tool for your growth when used wisely.

So, are you ready to go with me on a journey with 2 imaginary but real characters in this real world and witness my story of self-discovery.

I am sure my story will inspire you to find your true self and live a bold life.

Source - https://www.nimh.nih.gov/health/publications/social-anxiety-disorder-more-than-just-shyness

The Hidden Cost of Fear

Let's talk about the elephant in the room: fear. It's one of those things we all know is there, lurking in the background, yet we rarely address it head-on. But fear has a hidden weight, a burden we carry without even realising it, and it's often much heavier than we ever imagine.

The fear of judgement, specifically, acts like an invisible cage. It holds us back, whispers doubts in our ears, and keeps us from stepping into opportunities at every stage of life. And where does it all start? We pick it up as we grow, from family, friends, and society. We learn to fear what others might think, and before we know it, we've fallen into a trap that follows us into adulthood.

Let me hit you with some eye-opening facts: A study from the University of Wisconsin-Madison found that 30% of high school and college students don't participate in class because of social anxiety. That's right—almost one in 3 students stays silent, not because they don't know the answer, but because they're afraid of being judged. This fear doesn't just affect their grades; it limits their potential and future opportunities.

Think about that for a moment—the doors that stay closed simply because someone is too scared to speak up.

The National Institute of Mental Health also reports that 73% of people experience crippling anxiety when speaking in front of others. This doesn't just impact school presentations; it carries over into the workplace, limiting promotions and career advancement. LinkedIn even shows that 41% of Americans feel anxious about something as simple as submitting a resume. Imagine missing out on job opportunities because the fear of rejection holds you back from even applying.

And it's not just students and professionals feeling the weight of judgement. According to NAMI, up to 60% of individuals with mental health challenges avoid seeking help because they're scared of how others might react. Fear of being judged keeps them suffering in silence when they could be getting the support they need.

The truth is fear of judgement isn't just a personal problem – it's universal. It doesn't care about your age, nationality, or social status. And it's stealing opportunities, dreams, and progress from all of us. So maybe it's time we stopped letting it run the show.

Let's confront it, talk about it and, most importantly, begin to break free from its grip.

sources

1. LinkedIn, 2023

2. APA, "2023 Work in America Survey," conducted by The Harris Poll, April 17–27, 2023

3. NAMI: Mental Health by the Numbers Study 2023

Part One

Meet Mr Bliss and Mr Blameworth –
Two Voices Within Us

Before we start talking, let's meet the 2 most fictional characters of our personality - Mr Bliss and Mr Blameworth.

What to say about them, both are the most critical parts of our personalities that define our lives, make us feel how we feel, and our behaviour and actions are largely influenced by them. They are the entities that shape us based on the circumstances, situations, and environment around us.

Imagine you are walking down the path of life with 2 critics by your side, one is Mr Bliss who is the voice of optimism, self-assurance and contentment. He is the cheerleader for you who celebrates you and your smaller and bigger wins and makes every challenge easier to handle.

On the other side, meet Mr Blameworth, who is the shadow of self-doubt and criticism; he will always point fingers at you, criticise you for all the mistakes, and create only fear of all kinds.

Both are responsible for the continuous chatter and hypercritical discussions in our mind.

Mr Bliss and Mr Blameworth help us define our personality based on what we learn, what we go through, and what we experience. Our self-image is shaped by them within us.

Together, these 2 voices will shape your life and decide how we see ourselves during the journey and it's on us if we follow the lightness of Mr Bliss or will you be held back by the weight of Mr Blameworth's critique.

Now let me introduce them to you, as you will find them all the time with us.

Mr Bliss – The Cheerleader of Your Life

Mr Bliss is a good person, or I can say, he is the positive and virtuous side of our personality.

Mr Bliss is the empathetic, optimistic, honest, compassionate, wise, patient, courageous, balanced, and grateful person in all of us who always motivates us with positive thoughts and ideas.

Mr Bliss is the inner joy and goodness in us. He is the guiding force of positivity and happiness in us.

He is the one who always tells us not to worry in any situation. He is the one who inspires us to do bigger things and tries to make us happy in every circumstance.

He is the one who tries to show us the light at the end of the tunnel in every situation in life. When you feel low in life, she is the one who tells you, "Dude, this is just a situation, everything will be fine."

When you think life is difficult and wonder why this is happening to me only, then he is the one who says, "Dude, this is fine, everyone has these situations in life and these situations only make us learn and strong."

Mr Bliss is in all of us, and he is listening to you and smiling now when you are reading or thinking something good or positive.

Imagine the most beautiful person you can encounter in this universe, and that person is Mr Bliss. (You all can give him a face with your imagination)

Mr Blameworth – The Critic of Your Life

Mr Blameworth is the bad person who acts as an inner critic or negative inner voice in all of us.

He is the one who makes us feel small, fearful, anxious, and disgusted in almost every situation.

Mr Blameworth is insensitive, selfish, self-centred, discouraging, impatient, cruel, foolish, ignorant, harsh, unforgiving, impulsive, weak-willed, discontented, greedy and many other negative characteristics.

He is the one who makes us impulsive, negative, and feel imbalanced.

Mr Blameworth is the person in us who judges us the most and keeps reminding us of our issues. He is the one who keeps telling us that things are not good with you and people must be thinking in the wrong way.

He is the one who doesn't allow us to feel happy about many things and keeps reminding us of our problems.

Now, when we move forward, we will see how both impact our life and mindset. So, make friends with them for the whole journey here through this book.

Please Remember

Both Mr Bliss and Mr Blameworth are real personalities living inside you, and you have the power to decide who you'll nurture a deeper bond with.

By choosing to connect more with Mr Bliss, your inner cheerleader, you will invite optimism, self-confidence, and growth in life.

On the other hand, if you focus more on Mr Blameworth, your inner critic, you invite negativity, the fear of judgement, and a ton of self-doubt.

Both serve a purpose, but it's your decision who plays a bigger role in shaping your path. And in understanding that both the cheerleader and critic can add value to your life and inspire you to grow.

Part Two

Let's Decode the Anatomy of Judgement

Behind The Masks: Unveiling the Fear and the Judgement - Let's Understand the Psychology of this Fear and the Judgement

Let's understand the basics now and find out why we develop this fear in the first place.

This starts when we are kids, and our brain starts developing patterns of how we respond to different situations, like fear or anxiety.

We start observing and learning about the world around us, and this starts with our house, family, and parents when we are kids. You know the name responsible for this is the Amygdala, which works like the brain's alarm system that becomes active when we encounter something that feels scary, unfamiliar, and uncomfortable. This can be as simple as something like a loud noise, a new place, or meeting a stranger. Whenever our friend Amygdala senses any probable danger, it triggers a fear response and makes our body ready to run away, fight, or freeze.

Meanwhile, the hippocampus, which is responsible for creating memories, begins to connect these experiences to a specific feeling. Let's walk through it: as a child, whenever I faced dogs, my parents and family asked me to get away immediately and created a sense of fear that the dog could bite me. So, my hippocampus stored dogs with fear, and this led me to feel anxious whenever I saw a dog around me (not anymore). This is how our brain prepares us and creates patterns from our childhood for our responses and behaviour. If a child is frequently experiencing stressful situations, the brain might become more sensitive to anxiety.

And now the reverse: if a child has more positive experiences, if parents and family always allow and inspire the child whenever he is experiencing something new, then the child will have better resilience and the brain is better trained to manage fear, anxiety, and any adverse situations.

So, this is the basic reason and patterns of fear or anxiety in our life.

Now, let me take you to my story, which is not uncommon. This is the typical childhood of people of my age (pls don't ask my age now 😊).

I have seen my parents, family, and people around me quite sensitive and stressful in situations where there was no need to feel that way. I had seen that during my entire childhood. Obviously, I do not blame them for this behaviour as it was natural and something they have experienced throughout their life. I don't think in the 90s parenting was ever such an important topic to be discussed, unlike now.

Our brain is learning what we see around and prepares us with automatic reflexes in entire life, so it's important to understand that nothing happens suddenly. The fear or anxiety is a response which has developed over the years for us.

The fear of judgement is a process of

- Noticing (first when we see, hear or experience something that catches our attention
- Thinking (think about what we notice)
- Feeling (feel about what we think and it can be multiple emotions like anger, happiness or concern)
- Deciding (after thinking and feeling about the situation), acting (now we may act based on our findings) and finally
- Looking back (now we might reflect on our decision and also save the learning for next time in the similar situation).

So, next time if someone judges you, then understand that this is the response of our upbringing or surroundings and have empathy for that person instead of taking things personally I am sure it's clear that this fear of judgement is the result of multiple experiences accumulated inside people.

Psychology of Fear: Now, if we talk about the basic psychology of the fear of judgement, there are multiple reasons for it; however, the most common ones are:

Social Connection and Approval: Driven by the human need and the fear of rejection.

It's a human need and from ages, as human beings, we are wired to seek connection and approval from others, which starts with immediate family, friends, and eventually society. Social connection gives us a sense of safety and identity.

The fear of judgement is quite close to the fear of rejection. Most of the time, we worry about whether others are judging us negatively, and this impacts how we behave with ourselves and others.

Self-esteem and Self-worth: Sometimes external validation comes with a mask of self-worth, and we tie our worth with how people perceive us. Trust me, this is the biggest trap we have around us that we need to break. This fear is found irrespective of anyone's social status or success.

Now, another big trap we see around is "Perfectionism" – for some people, being a perfectionist means doing everything right so they can avoid criticism from others, and it's high time we accept this.

Past experiences – in most cases, this fear comes from our childhood influences such as how we were treated by people around us, how we were criticised by our parents, teachers, or friends. And in the case of friends, many a times it's also trauma and bullying that shape this emotion and push us into this trap.

Overthinking and False Mind-reading: Sometimes we do a lot in some situations and we start believing how people must be thinking about us and often assuming the worst-case scenario (which most of the time is baseless) keeps us trapped.

I remember my friend "Pooja" today, who was a talented graphic designer; she was magical with great imaginative power. I have not met anyone like her in my life. She was bright, but because we were in a town called "Jamshedpur or Tata Nagar," she needed bigger motivation to make her dream a reality, and in the 90s, the internet was not common for common people like us. Suddenly, while we were suggesting her to pursue her dream, she asked to connect with some people who could help her, and coincidentally, she met her cousins who were ready to help her work towards it. Unfortunately, she was paralysed by the fear of judgement, and she kept imagining how people could criticise her for her bad designs and talk bad about her, and eventually, family may scold her for wasting money on doing something she was not capable of. This perceived fear never allowed her to work for her dream. Today, she is a homemaker who is dying every day thinking, "I wish I had pursued my dream; I wish I had pushed myself more." and she feels less worthy thinking this all the time.

This is not just a story but a lesson for all who can't push themselves beyond this fear and do something for their dreams.

Pooja's story is a good reality checkpoint of how this false trap can limit your life and leave you with a lifetime regret of not trying something you should have.

The fear of judgement is deeply rooted with a strong desire to feel accepted and a strong fear of rejection

And today's social media is making it more lethal, and we should be careful about it.

Judgement

Now, let's understand the fanciest word that you are going to hear now and then: Judgement

Judgement is a constant evaluation of things, right or wrong, good or bad. We live in a situation where everyone is evaluating everything around them.

People evaluate us, and we evaluate people based on how they look, what they wear, how they behave, and talk. We all interpret everything around us with our own eyes and belief system, irrespective of reality.

We judge everything based on our own self-perception and past experiences.

I am not saying judgement is always wrong, but for the right judgement, you need the right mindset ☺

Judgement is just a double-edged sword, and it can be beneficial and dangerous at the same time, and it's on us (our own Mr Bliss and Mr Blameworth) to decide how to use it.

Now let's see how Mr Bliss and Mr Blameworth can use this as a good or bad tool for you.

If Mr Bliss is using this tool, then this helps you in making:

- Informed decisions – good judgement can help you make the right decisions with careful consideration and analysis in any situation.

- Troubleshooting - Good judgement allows you to access complex situations and can foresee potential problems, and can provide you with an effective solution.

- Protective – Can keep you safe by helping recognise and avoid risky situations in life.

- Moral compass – Can help deal with ethical dilemmas, keeping you aligned with your values and principles, helping to save integrity and responsibility.

- Good judgement helps you judge situations with empathy, which allows for more compassionate relationships and life.

Now, when Mr Blameworth uses this tool of judgement, this brings:

- Biases and prejudice – Bad judgement often brings personal biases and stereotypes leading to unfair behaviour and decisions.

- Instant decisions – Sometimes Mr. Blameworth can push you for a quicker decision without analysing the situation or with adequate information can lead to mistakes and poor results.

- Arrogance – it's nothing but misguided confidence.

- Stress and Anxiety – Excessive self-judgement and worrying about what others think can lead to the unfavourable situation of stress and anxiety.

Judgement is a habit, which becomes a system of our subconscious mind and can be seen in our behaviour.

Here is how it works:

When we frequently make judgements about people, situations, or ourselves, these judgements reinforce neural pathways in our brain. The more we do this, it becomes automatic, so with repetition and reinforcement, the habit to judge becomes a part of life and starts happening almost reflexively.

Cognitive Biases (cognitive biases are like "thinking traps" that affect how we interpret and respond to the world around us, often without us realising it) are another reason that strengthens the habit of judging and reinforces habitual judgemental thinking.

Societal Taming – From a young age, our family, surroundings, media, movies, and societal norms expose us to this judgemental mindset, and we keep judging others, sometimes also to gain approval.

For instance, if you have grown up in surroundings where people criticise others quite often, then you would also start doing that to seek approval. So, stop blaming yourself for the bad habit and try to be friends with your Mr Bliss.

Emotional Reaction – Most of the time, we become judgemental because of our emotional state of mind. For instance, if you are insecure, envious, or fearful, you will always judge people reflecting your own insecurity.

A Closer Peek – Imagine you're scrolling through social media, and you see a post of a colleague on vacation, looking carefree and happy. If you're feeling a bit insecure about your own life or career, you might react by thinking, "She's so irresponsible, taking so much time off! Who even has time for vacations like that?" This judgement isn't really about her; it's a reflection of your own insecurity or stress. If you were feeling content and secure, you'd likely just think, "Good for her, that looks fun!" or even feel inspired to plan your own trip.

A False Sense of Security – Sometimes being too judgemental can give you a sense of control and a false sense of security.

A Closer Peek – Imagine you're working in a team, and you find yourself frequently judging a particular coworker's work, thinking things like, "They don't know what they're doing; their ideas are weak." You may feel that by mentally putting their work down, you're reassuring yourself that your own work is better or that you're in control. This judgement creates a "false sense of security," where you believe you're safe from criticism or failure because you feel superior.

In reality, this mindset doesn't add any true security. It's actually holding you back from collaborating effectively and improving your own skills. By letting go of harsh judgements and instead focusing on constructive feedback or teamwork, you can find real confidence based on growth rather than a false sense of security and superiority.

Breaking this habit of judgement is a conscious effort, and it requires awareness and strong willpower to challenge and change.

Judgement is the process of forming an opinion about someone's decisions based on your own questionable decisions.

Judgement is our ability to give a verdict on someone else's choices from the comfort of our own messy existence.

Judgement can be a powerful tool when used thoughtfully and constructively and equally dangerous when used without much reflection.

Chapter 2

The Power of Our Inner Critic

This is one of the most powerful aspects of our life that shapes us and our personality and life.

The inner critic can be both positive and negative, but most of the time it's negative, pushing us into this judgement trap.

The inner critic often amplifies the fear of judgement from others, making us second guess our actions and decisions. If we talk about the origin of the inner critic, it comes from childhood influences and social conditioning. Nowadays, we can also blame social media, which often amplifies this by constantly presenting idealised versions of life.

It's story time – During my early days in Mumbai, juggling a demanding career and raising my elder daughter, Zyana, I often found myself scrolling through social media during rare breaks. I'd see posts of other working mothers who seemed to have it all—a spotless home, perfectly groomed kids, and thriving careers. These curated snapshots made me feel inadequate, even though I was achieving so much.

I remember one post vividly: a mom hosting an elaborate birthday party for her child. Instantly, guilt crept in, and I thought, "I could never pull that off with my hectic schedule. Am I failing as a mother?" At the time, I didn't realise those posts were just highlights, not the full picture.

Over time, as I became more self-aware, I realised that even my own life could look idealised if someone only saw the bright moments I chose to share. This understanding helped me stop letting those fleeting images define my worth and focus on the meaningful connections and successes I was building in real life.

That experience taught me how social media amplifies judgement and insecurity, making us compare our behind-the-scenes reality to someone else's highlights. It was a powerful reminder to step back and see the bigger picture.

Now, you have met both Mr Bliss and Mr Blameworth. Both are a part of all of you.

Mr Bliss is your motivator for life who pushes you to strive for excellence, who asks you to learn from mistakes and keep moving.

Mr Bliss is the person who tells you, "you can do better", "keep working hard", "learn from mistakes", "don't worry about what others are thinking", "focus on improving it", "you are bright and can do magical things", "you are born to do something big in life", "you can bring a change", "nothing is impossible, just try", "don't listen to people who bring you down", "you have started it so keep doing and don't stop", "you have handled challenges like this and you can also handle it now", "It's okay to fall or lose, learning is important", "It's okay not to be perfect, you are doing your best", "Take a break and begin again", "you have the strength to succeed and make this possible", "you should take this risk" - can you talk to your Mr Bliss now?

Mr Bliss is inside us; we all hear his voice from time to time, and let me tell you, the more you listen to him, the better for you. Talk to him every day when you wake up and discuss your situation; most of the time, he can give you the solutions you are looking for outside (it's a secret revealed 😊))

Appreciate Mr Bliss and thank him for helping you in difficult times when you didn't even ask for it, be kind to him and thank him for encouraging you. Express gratitude to him for being a part of the journey.

Now, let's meet Mr Blameworth, who is defining problems for you, who is harsh and has a judgemental voice. He is the one who talks about your flaws, mistakes, and insecurities most of the time.

It's Mr Blameworth who tells you, "you are not good enough", "why are you even trying, you can't do this", "what others will tell if you fail in this", "people will laugh at you", "if it's not perfect, it's worthless", "shit, you made this mistake, you ruined everything", "what do you think of yourself, if you fail in this everyone will laugh", "don't take this risk, you will definitely fail", "others are better than you", "no one cares about you", "do you deserve this", "we can do it later, just postpone", "you are a burden to others, why do you do this all the time", "beware of change, you won't be able to adjust to it", "you should be ashamed of yourself for doing this", "only a smart person can do this, why do you even try", "you are too old for this or too young for this, forget about it", "people are pretending, they actually hate you behind your back", "you are too sensitive, tumse nahi hoga", "you don't deserve this, idiot", "you are just wasting your time, nothing is going to happen, etc. and etc. Isn't it rude ☹️?

Yes, it's extremely rude and judgemental, and this is exactly how Mr Blameworth acts and talks inside us. It's him who is stopping you from attaining greatness, it's him who is pulling you down before anyone else does. However, it also helps in retrospection and then finally Mr Bliss takes over and gives direction/determination to correct things/issues which Mr Blameworth has highlighted.

He is the first person who can bully you, so don't give access to Mr Blameworth. Respect yourself before you ask from others.

Now, let me give you some snapshot of people who could silence Mr Blameworth within and listen to Mr Bliss.

A popular real life tale of J.K. Rowling, who is one of the world-famous authors today with Harry Potter, faced similar challenges with her inner critic. She was a single mother, suffering from depression, and her story on Harry Potter was rejected by 12 publishers before being accepted. Rowling has spoken openly about her self-doubt and fear of failure and emphasised overcoming the inner critic if one must live for the dream. (Source - BBC - J.K. Rowling: How she overcame rejection and became a bestseller)

Another popular personality from India is Sudha Chandran who was a vibrant and talented classical dancer, but at the age of 16, she met with an accident and lost one of her legs. This could have been the end of her dancing career, but Mr Bliss inside her refused to give up and constantly pushed her to believe in herself. Don't you think Mr Blameworth within her must have tried to stop her by being hard, rude and negative, but rather, she chose to follow Mr Bliss and she returned to the stage, defying all the odds and created history like never before.

There are multiple scenarios which can demonstrate that it's you who must choose between the Blameworth and Bliss within you and give it a direction.

By managing our inner critics (Mr Bliss and Mr Blameworth), we can reduce the fear of judgement and embrace opportunities with more confidence.

The point is not to silence Mr Blameworth, but to transform him into Mr Bliss and redirect life towards positivity, and its easier said than done. This needs practice, but it's possible.

Chapter 3

The Quite Thunder – Decoding Anxiety - Understanding Anxiety or Social Phobia Due to The Fear of Judgement

Post discussion what this fear is and how it works, now let's talk about how we can feel this fear as anxiety or social phobia.

Social anxiety or social phobia has become a significant problem in our society. And this is not an age-specific issue. This can happen to anyone irrespective of their age, and it's a more sensitive topic than we perceive.

In medical terms, this is called "social anxiety disorder," which is dangerous for one's mental wellbeing.

This is anxiety or fear due to society and it's a deep-rooted issue which arises from the fear of being negatively judged, criticised, or rejected by others in any social situations.

And this can be seen generally in any social situation where someone is feeling embarrassed or making silly mistakes in front of others, and it's not only limited to the social situations but can include the fear of societal norms, expectations and pressure.

Many of us with social phobia may feel like, "I am not fit for social gatherings," or "I am not like them," or "I am not fitting with their standard."

This is one thing; I suffered the most, and this can make you feel extremely miserable in any situation.

I have grown up in a middle-class family, where my family was always bothered about what others are thinking or how we should behave so that others shouldn't think or talk badly bad about us, and the people who really contributed to making me phobic were my extended family.

I am born and brought up in a city called Jamshedpur or Tata Nagar, where we had my mom's cousins and their families in the same city, and I don't remember a day when they didn't judge us for everything possible.

My father was earning reasonably well, which was only sufficient to give us basic, non-fancy, and uncomplicated life. Being the eldest child in my family, I had to face the hurdles before my siblings would.

I was always a very aspirational girl who wanted to do something bigger in life, wanted to do something extraordinary, but had no wings, as I was going to a Hindi medium school run by a Punjabi community trust, where academics often took a backseat. At the same time, my other family members were living a slightly fancier life with bigger schools and other facilities, but I was happy with whatever we had and could see the multiple issues my parents had to curb their desire to fulfil their child's requirement.

I remember how my close relatives tortured us by comparing me with others and making me feel useless most of the time (without realising they were doing that).

Let's look back at an incident – story time.

I still remember one particular family gathering vividly. My cousin, who was studying at one of the best English medium schools in Jamshedpur, walked into the room, confidently speaking English and dressed in the latest fashion trends. Everyone seemed in awe of her. Then they turned to me.

One of my uncles laughed and said, "Look at her – she's so polished. And you? Always wearing such plain clothes. Maybe you should take some tips from her." Another relative chimed in, mocking my Hindi accent when I tried to say a phrase in English, making everyone laugh.

At that moment, I felt so small and out of place, like no matter how hard I tried, I'd never measure up. They didn't mean to hurt me, perhaps thinking their comments were harmless, but they unknowingly chipped away at my confidence. These constant comparisons made me question my worth and abilities, even though I was doing my best in my circumstances.

Looking back, I've realised that their words reflected their own biases and limited understanding, not my true potential. But at the time, it felt like I was stuck in a never-ending cycle of judgement.

This had the worst impact on my life. I threw myself into a deep sense of insecurity and inferiority complex. This must have happened to most of the people of my age during the 90s.

I remember clearly the suffering I had during my teenage and later part of life. I never got the confidence to feel like many and clearly suffered with this social phobia which was created by people around me. I can still see the impact on me.

However, it would be unfair not to mention that I now realise I was overthinking about how others perceived me. I constantly restricted myself, creating a version of the situation in my mind that was far more exaggerated and overwhelming than the reality.

Now, I realise that I wish I hadn't thought much about people around me and would have lived that golden period joyfully.

This is not just my story, but many around us in the middle class family, where parents work hard to keep their child at par with the world but their close relatives do not understand their pain and limitations

This fear is not real; it's an exaggerated view of our mind that impacts how we think, how we feel, and how we behave in any social situation.

And we can witness this in many forms, like:

- Too much self-consciousness – we overthink that everyone is only looking at us and behave differently in any social situation.

- Avoidance – most of the time we avoid gathering due to fear of being judged and criticised with feelings of self-doubt or uncertainty or fear of looking stupid, silly, or boring.

- Physical symptoms like sweating, trembling, rapid heartbeat, nausea, sweaty palms, dry throat, stomach ache, or light-headedness, etc.

- An urge to get out of the situation.

- A negative thought like "I am making a fool of myself" or "I don't fit here or don't belong here", "why is everyone looking at me only" etc.

Social phobia can be more dangerous than we think. A person with this phobia would like to avoid a range of situations like:

- Parties or get-togethers

- Presentations or public speaking

- To start a conversation

- Voicing an opinion

- Meeting someone new for the first time

- Dating

- Shopping

- Talking to seniors or higher members of the family

- Any situation with a spotlight, etc.

Now, tell me if anyone can avoid these situations in life and have no impact.

I have seen people avoiding these situations in the name of being shy or being an introvert ☺, but social anxiety, introversion, and shyness are different things.

Introversion is a personality trait, and social anxiety is a mental health condition. There are introverts who love partying and meeting new people without any fear of judgement.

I have a close relative, Tanu who is a student, who is young, energetic, and creative but naturally introverted. However, when she's with her close friends or comfort group, she transforms into the life of the party—an introvert who feels completely free and unafraid of judgement. There can be multiple sources of this fear, such as some psychological roots as we discussed before. It can be conditioning from childhood or some cognitive issues.

Chapter 4

Shades of fear – The Unseen Burden

Let's dig in and explore the impacts of this fear of judgement on our daily lives, from relationships to personal life to professional life and on health.

This is a ridiculous feeling in case, you have never been in this situation. It's scary to feel judged, and this feeling can make someone sad, incomplete, like something is missing syndrome and eventually leaves feeling left out or depressed (and I had this emotion for a major part of life.

The feeling of being judged makes you feel different with low self-esteem and low confidence, and this is the biggest issue I have observed around me, especially among the grown-ups and adolescents.

Research done by PMC (Pub Med Central, one of the most relevant health research institutions) in 2023[1] on the data on self-esteem among the adolescents in India.

The research was done with 600 adolescents from higher secondary schools and colleges aged between 13 and 19. They found that 70% of them had a poor level of self-esteem, while 30% had a moderate level of self-esteem. The good part was that post-intervention assertiveness training, the results changed positively.

Source 1 (Bioinformation. 2023; 19(11): 1086–1089. Published online 2023 Nov 30. doi: 10.6026/973206300191086)

The fear of judgement may be a small topic to be addressed, but it can have a complicated and varied impact on our day-to-day life without us realising it.

Let's begin with the first impact of the deep-rooted and magnificent impact.

1. The psychological impact – the fear of being judged which we normally carry from childhood can lead to low self-esteem, self-respect, or confidence. This makes us critical of ourselves, fearing that others will judge us harshly for our mistakes.

    During my childhood, I vividly remember the fear of being judged, shaping so much of who I thought I was. One incident stands out: during a school debate competition, I knew the answers and had rehearsed my points, but the fear of stumbling over words in English stopped me from raising my hand. I imagined the whole class laughing, whispering, and judging me for every small mistake. Instead of giving it a try, I stayed silent, letting the moment pass.

    That fear didn't just stay in the classroom. It followed me into adulthood, making me second-guess my abilities at work, avoiding risks, and constantly criticising myself. I believed that if I wasn't perfect, I'd be judged harshly, just as I had feared in my younger days. It took years—and plenty of self-reflection—to realise that those fears were exaggerated. We can normally feel this as various emotions like anxiety disorder, depression, and chronic stress.

The National Institute of Mental Health states that social anxiety disorder, driven by fear of judgement, affects approximately 15 million adults in the US, making it the third most common mental health issue today, after chronic stress and adverse experiences.

2. Isolation and loneliness - The fear of judgement can cause people to withdraw from social situations and lead to loneliness and isolation.

3. Missing out on opportunities – this fear can make you lose out on many opportunities not only in the workplace for advancements, and why I am talking about this first because I have witnessed this a lot. In the beginning of my career, I suffered with this issue and lost a hell of a lot of chances to grow. I remember myself never talking in meetings, fear in sharing ideas. Oh my God, this was the worst feeling. Most of the time in meetings, I used to have multiple ideas and points to share but never used to share with this fear and by the end of the meeting, I always used to feel awful about being unable to talk. The worst part was that people with low-worth ideas used to get a lot of applause, which made me think for days, "I wish I would have shared this in meetings or I wish I would have spoken this." I have gone through this feeling multiple times over many years and this feels awful, so never do this in your life. Speak up when you feel like it, speak up if you feel you can add something relevant (or irrelevant sometimes, and there are a hell of a lot of people who speak because they want to talk irrespective of relevance 😊) and according to a LinkedIn survey, 85% of professionals hesitate to share their ideas in the workplace due to fear of judgement, which can limit their career growth.

I have also suffered in my personal life with this issue, when I need to ask something from someone, sometimes even from my father. I needed a lot of guts.

Another situation, which happens with most of us is when someone says something wrong to you and you don't respond to that person with the right answer or comment during the conversation, and this leaves you with the feeling, "Yaar I should have spoken this or Maine aisa kyun nai bola." And this thought troubles you a lot later. So, speak up if you feel like, this will save. You from mental agony and reliving the conversation.

4. Talking in public – The fear of judgement has one of the worst impacts on talking in public, and it can be a small birthday party or a boardroom presentation. I remember this issue was so dominant for me that I used to avoid attending birthday parties or any party because I might have to speak there, or people may ask me to dance, sing, or do any other thing where I was not comfortable. I wasn't comfortable doing anything. Oh, I have goosebumps thinking about it now because I wasted a hell of a lot of opportunities to celebrate and be happy with people around me. And this is still an issue for many of us. If you are reading this and have this problem, then please get out of this because.

Let me share a truth: It took me over 30 years to grasp—no one is thinking about you as much as you think they are. People are far too busy managing their own impressions, caught in their own loops of 'What will others think?' to spend time dwelling on you. So, here's my advice: don't waste your precious time worrying about being judged. Instead, use that energy to focus on becoming the best version of yourself.

5. **Something is missing syndrome** – The fear of judgement can always make someone feel like something is missing or something is wrong with me, and this feeling can create a persistent situation of distress or chronic stress and anxiety and always make us feel under pressure.

    Story Time - In my early twenties, I found myself constantly battling the nagging thought that I wasn't "enough." This feeling hit its peak during my time in Vishakhapatnam, where everything about me seemed wrong—my accent, my simple clothes, and my hesitant attempts at English. I vividly remember an incident when I had to deliver a presentation in front of my classmates. My heart raced, and my palms were clammy as I stood in front of them, feeling utterly out of place.

    Despite preparing for days, all I could think was, what if they laugh at my pronunciation? What if I stumble over my words? That fear consumed me. I felt as though there was a glaring deficiency in me, something everyone could see but I couldn't fix.

    After delivering the presentation – surprisingly, without any major blunders – I still didn't feel relief. Instead, I left the room with that same haunting thought: Something must be wrong with me. This invisible burden didn't just weigh on my confidence; it trickled into every aspect of my life, creating a constant state of stress and self-doubt.

6. Social media influence - Looking back, I can't help but feel grateful that we didn't have the overwhelming presence of social media in the 90s. Everyone's realising now how consuming it can be, but back then, life felt simpler, less scrutinised, and far less overwhelming. Nowadays platforms like Facebook or Instagram intensify the fear of judgement, and people constantly feel they

are being compared or comparing themselves with the ideal picture, vacation, or position, and all. There are many surveys and research studies that show people feel pressured to present a perfect picture of themselves due to social media influence.

Story Time – There was a time in my career when I felt like I was always running late to the party of success. Every time I opened social media, it seemed like everyone I knew was sprinting ahead – promotions, exotic vacations, awards. My feed was a highlight reel of achievements, and I couldn't help but compare my life to theirs.

I convinced myself that I was falling behind, stuck in a no-growth zone. The constant barrage of perfectly curated lives made me feel inadequate as if I needed to do more and be more. I started questioning my choices, my pace, and even my worth. I wasn't chasing my dreams anymore; I was chasing the need to keep up with the world's version of success.

But here's what I didn't see at that time: while I was busy envying filtered snapshots of other people's lives, I was missing out on the unfiltered beauty of my own. I wasn't behind; I was missing the joy of the life I already had—giggling with my daughters, those silly tea sessions with my husband, and even the small wins at work that went unnoticed because they weren't "Insta-worthy."

Social media had tricked me into believing that growth was only real if it was visible. The truth? Growth is silent, slow, and deeply personal. I wasn't missing out on success—I was missing out on living.

Here's my lesson: don't let the urge to highlight your achievements rob you of the joy of living a real, unfiltered life. No post or reel can ever replace the quiet contentment of knowing you're exactly where you're meant to be.

7. **Low on life satisfaction ratio** - The feeling of being judged can reduce overall quality of life. This reduces the happiness quotient and the satisfaction ratio, which has a direct impact on life. This may make people feel stuck in something or with someone, or that things are not fair with them, or why this is happening to me kind of feelings, which can leave you unrested.

Sneak peek time – There was a time when the fear of judgement quietly drained my happiness. I remember walking through the office parking lot, seeing sleek cars, and hearing colleagues boast about their fancy titles. It triggered a constant loop of comparison: Why don't I have that? Why am I not there yet? Am I not enough?

This mindset chipped away at my satisfaction, making me feel stuck and unfairly treated. But then it hit me – the fancy cars and big titles didn't define success or happiness. I was missing out on appreciating my own journey and blessings, which most of us do. We forget how we started our journey and how long we have already reached it.

When I shifted my focus from what I lacked to what I had, the unrest faded, and I began to feel truly content. The real win isn't about keeping up; it's about finding joy in your own story.

The fear of judgement is a universal challenge, something we all face at some point in our lives. Its impact on the quality of life is immediate and undeniable, often holding us back from reaching our true potential. But here's the good news: it doesn't have to be this way.

This book is your guide to breaking free from the judgement trap. Going forward, you'll discover practical tips and actionable techniques to overcome this fear and reclaim your authentic self. Let's take this journey together – because your best life is waiting on the other side.

Chapter 5

Navigating Social Situations and Cultural Judgement - Uncovering the Roots of the Fear

Imagine this: every time you walk into a room full of people—whether it's a party, a meeting, or even a family gathering—you can feel the silent eyes on you. You start second-guessing your outfit, your words, even your body language.

Most of us have very likely faced these situations at some point in our lives, regardless of age or circumstances, making us vulnerable to societal pressures and high expectations. Undue societal pressure and perceived high expectations create the fear of judgement in us.

Sneak Peek Time – I still vividly remember the first time I attended a high-profile corporate meeting early in my career. The room was filled with senior leaders, all impeccably dressed, confident, and poised. As I walked in, it felt like every eye turned to me. My heart raced, and an inner dialogue began: Is my outfit too plain? Should I have worn something more formal? What if I say something wrong? What will they think of me?

When it was my turn to speak, my voice trembled as I tried to deliver my points. Even though I had prepared thoroughly, I couldn't focus—I was too busy analysing how I might be coming across. Were they judging my ideas, my tone, my appearance?

Looking back now, I realise that most of the "silent eyes" I felt weren't real. Everyone in that room was preoccupied with their own presentations, their own impressions, and their own fears. The pressure I felt was largely self-imposed, fuelled by societal expectations and my own fear of judgement.

That day taught me a valuable lesson: the fear of judgement often exists more in our minds than in reality. Recognising this is the first step toward breaking free from its grip and showing up authentically, no matter the setting. The fear is more than just fear of making a mistake or failing; it is also fear of the subsequent judgement that my error carries. Judgements like "I must seem incompetent", "She must be weird", or "He must be socially awkward". I can see the judgement clouding their eyes - but I see the judgement because I expect it, as there is a certain amount of pressure to conform (to be socially the same).

The societal pressure to act a certain way pushes us into that invisible box, and if we don't want to do/talk/act in a "normal" way, we slowly suppress parts of our character, opinions (or there may be topics we won't sign up for), or humanity (i.e., we don't cite our art/depart from "professional" now instead of "normal" behaviour) to simply "go with it" or we act against the norm and are punished by being viewed as "the one" who acts differently, one who doesn't belong.

Judgement also has some amount of cultural meaning in the sense that living in a society has taught you the unspoken laws of how to behave, what you should believe/do - who you should be.

Cultures create moulds for people, and our cultural moulds say: don't be too loud, don't be different. We learn (absorb) those cultural moulds and become those moulds, and changing/moving outside of that mould of yourself brings attention (stares, whispers, labels) you weren't ready to wear.

I remember when I was growing up, my mom and other relatives used to say, "Don't laugh too much; otherwise, your teeth will be bigger and odd, and nobody will marry you." My lips were quite full, and I remember my mom saying in a stressful voice, "Who will marry you with these thick lips?" And then now when I see women in the film industry go for plastic surgery for their full lips, I think, "Why the hell did I waste my life thinking just the opposite?" And then I also realise that society sometimes judges you on things That they are not themselves sure about.

And so, the judgement can then snowball as a result of cultural pressures that can be exacerbated by fear, but rarely is discussed openly, but we experience the same internal strife.

Avoiding social interactions means losing touch with who we truly are. It makes us afraid to express ourselves, share our views, or handle opinions that go against what society expects.

To conform to those standards means punishing ourselves for just being us.

Let's discuss some of the roots of fear around us, which hold us back from being our true selves.

1. Middle-Class Syndrome and the Pressure to Prove

You must be thinking, why the middle-class syndrome because I bet that most of you reading this belong here or have risen from the middle class with your hard work and passion

It's the middle class who do the job of thinking about others, not the rich class or the underprivileged class. In fact, they are carefree when it comes to the fear of judgement; they are least bothered about people around them and always keep themselves at the centre of life, thinking, "What is in it for me, and why should I care about others?" I feel they are sorted here.

Sneak Peek Time – Fashion and trends are fascinating examples of how perceptions change over time. Take ripped jeans, for instance. Once a sign of poverty or hardship, they're now a global fashion statement, proudly worn by celebrities on red carpets and runways.

A similar shift happened when Anil Ambani, a prominent businessman, was spotted wearing mismatched sports shoes. What could have been seen as an odd or careless choice turned into a trend, celebrated as quirky and bold.

And the exact opposite happens to middle-class people.

For a middle-class society, society is always at the centre, and people keep thinking about how to impress the people around them so that they don't judge them, and this is the real trap.

I realised this issue when my parents and the whole family were more concerned about what others would think than what is right for us, what makes sense for us, or what we should do for ourselves. Being born into the middle class is like being born with societal and cultural expectations.

From the day you are born, society will keep you in a "Need to fit in" situation, and you keep struggling throughout your lifetime. Society will give you a predefined definition of success and respectability, and the day you are out of this "need to fit in" situation, you become successful. Now, let me explain this point in detail.

Every middle-class person is born with a "predefined mould" from parents, family, or society, which is typical: be a good student with good marks, get a good school, attend a good college, top the university, then find a good job, earn good money to pay taxes, provide for your family's basic needs, have some luxury, buy a house on loan, marry a good partner, have children, and then you fit into the predefined mould, setup, or trap. **REPEAT**... and the whole middle class operates within this so-called mould or trap.

I don't remember my parents or family asking me to do something that I like, something that makes me happy, something that I am passionate about. I am sure you get it now. It's always "do this so that people say good things about you" or "you get great appreciation." Now that I have lived half of my life, I refuse to let that hold any power over me. I wish I had realised it earlier in my life or had got a book like this.

This middle-class syndrome subtly imparts a sense of fear of judgement so that we can fit into this trap easily, and this is rooted so deeply that it has become a part of the middle-class DNA.

It's a trap which the government and banks design for the middle class because, for them, the middle class, "the average people or Aam Aadmi," are born to pay taxes so that can serve people above them and take care by paying for govt sponsored schemes for the people below them.

Now, if you look around the whole financial world, or fintech's are working to strengthen the middle-class trap. They want people to buy stuff on credit cards and want this population to live in a cycle of paycheck to paycheck, where savings are minimal, and wealth accumulation opportunities are minimal.

The irony of the middle class is that they have just enough to stay afloat, but never enough to break free.

The so-called middle class, which is called the backbone of the nation, where nowadays almost all the investors are putting a lot of money because they know that this class will only grow, because they are working hard to pay their bills, often finds itself trapped between aspirations and limitations. And these limitations are the fear of judgement or trying to fit in.

The typical society wants to earn enough to pay its bills and not enough to be financially free. Imagine we are fearful of them, just think why.

Why should you think of people who are least bothered about your growth, about your well-being.

This middle-class trap is a mindset that gives you poor vision or short-sightedness for your own life, makes you isolated because you are only busy in image management, and makes you complacent.

Heading typical ways this middle-class syndrome brings fear of judgement and impacts our ability to live an authentic life:

- **Pressure to fit in** – Anushka's Struggle to Fit In

   My friend Anushka grew up in a middle-class family with strong values. When she moved to Delhi for college, she felt out of place among her affluent, confident peers. They often teased her for being "too simple" and avoiding drinks or cigarettes at parties.

   One evening, someone casually said, "You're so boring, Anushka. You never try anything fun!" Fearing judgement and desperate to fit in, she gave in. Smoking and drinking became her way of blending in, even though she hated it.

It's a classic example of the pressure to meet societal standards, especially in middle-class families, where there's constant stress to "fit in" and be accepted, often at the cost of personal values.

- ***Avoid taking risks to avoid criticism or failure*** – The most annoying thing I have witnessed in the middle class is that they shy away from taking risks or pursuing any unconventional paths just to avoid the fear of making mistakes or being judged. People follow the same safe, predictable path and limit their true potential or passion.

Sneak Peek Time - Sid's Startup Dilemma

My friend Sid is brilliant. He's been toying with an innovative startup idea for years—one that could genuinely make a difference. But instead of diving into it, he's stuck in his comfortable 9-to-5 job, working tirelessly but without passion.

When I asked him why he wasn't taking the leap, he admitted, "What if it fails? Everyone will think I'm reckless for leaving a stable job. My family depends on me, and I can't let them down."

Sid's fear of judgement and failure keeps him tethered to the safety of a predictable routine. Like many in middle-class families, he's caught in the cycle of playing it safe, limiting himself and his dreams to avoid criticism.

- ***Making Judgement the Best Friend*** – From our childhood, we, the middle-class people, start comparing our children with relatives, putting the idea of external validation, which impacts all the decision-making we take in our life. So now you know the seed of this problem, and this makes us sensitive people with low self-esteem and confidence.

- ***Prioritising Others Before Us*** – From our childhood, we are made to prioritise others' opinions over our own desires, which suppresses our true self. This suppression not only diminishes our sense of confidence but also puts us in an inauthentic way.

Here, I can quote my current lifestyle that, despite earning well, my husband and I choose a frugal, grounded lifestyle. We value experiences over extravagance, but sometimes, society's whispers get loud: *"Are they struggling? Not doing well in life?"*

It makes us question and realise - whether we are living for ourselves or for others' expectations. This tug-of-war reminds me that true success isn't about proving anything; it's about living authentically, free from the judgement trap.

- ***Impact on personal growth*** – The fear of judgement often puts us in a comfort zone and stops us from exploring new opportunities, and here people stop living life to their full potential.

By addressing these roots of middle-class syndrome, we can treat ourselves and move towards living an authentic life.

Ask a few questions if you belong here and want to come out of this trap.

- Is chasing middle-class expectations holding you back from achieving something greater in life?

- Is your personal/financial/overall decision-making influenced by societal pressure to keep up with others?

- Are you trapped in the middle class because you are afraid to take risks or because people around you discourage you from doing so?

- Is society or the people around you holding you back with a lot of undue expectations?

- Are you living your true life or just trying to impress everyone around you?

Keep thinking. Meanwhile, we talk about other traps, and don't worry, you will get your answers here.

The middle-class trap is a mindset, and if you want to get out of this trap, then you need to change the mindset.

2. Introversion Anxiety or a Silent Struggle: The Fear of Disappearing or Being Invisible in the Crowd

Introversion is simply about preferring silence over chaos. It's about choosing relevance and comfort over noise and the spotlight. But introverts face a real challenge of the fear of being invisible in the crowd. It's more than just shyness; it's a much deep-rooted issue.

Why are we talking about this topic? Because it is less talked about and quite hidden in nature.

Introversion and anxiety are not the same thing, but it is a reality that anxiety is more commonly observed in introverts as a regular part of their life than in an extrovert or ambivert.

Anxiety is a silent chatter in your head, and most of the time it's Mr Blameworth who keeps reminding you of all your mistakes, guilts, and something that you must have done wrong 5 years back. Common, Mr Blameworth?

It's not only introverts who feel anxious chatter within, ambiverts and extroverts also feel it and suffer with it, but to a much lesser degree than introverts.

It's a silent struggle that can hamper one's self-esteem, self-confidence, and respect. Most of the time, we suffer from introversion anxiety and don't even know about it. Let me tell you a few symptoms with which you can relate. One thing is for sure, Mr Blameworth is more active than Mr Bliss in these situations.

1. You are overprepared for any circumstances – the first thought you get is the worst-case scenario, what if it doesn't work, and you tend to overprepare, like carrying your makeup in your handbag in case your luggage gets lost at the airport. You can see how this anxiety is making you overprepare and feel anxious at the same time.

2. The Yes trap – You are a people pleaser and can't say no to people.

    I remember a time when a colleague approached me with a last-minute request to help them prepare for an important presentation. I had a packed schedule that day, but I just couldn't bring myself to say no. After all, I didn't want to disappoint them or seem unhelpful.

    So, I stayed late, skipping dinner with my family and working well past midnight to meet my own deadlines after assisting them. The result? The presentation went smoothly, and they were grateful, but I was utterly drained—physically, emotionally, and mentally.

    This pattern repeated itself often, saying "yes" to everyone while quietly sacrificing my peace.

    It's a noble intention to want to help, but I learned the hard way that being a people pleaser comes at a steep cost – your own well-being. Sometimes, the kindest thing you can do for yourself, *and* others is to say no.

3. You talk more out of nervousness – sometimes you chat more only because you are nervous and want to look normal and cool about it.

4. You are never happy with your success – because whatever you do, Mr Blameworth is not allowing you to feel happy about it and pushing you harder and harder, so the actual issue is that "It's not enough ever."

5. Urge to prove yourself – I suffered with everything I am citing here, but this was the biggest one and this made me suffer terribly. I don't know why; I always had a feeling that I need to prove myself to this person or that person. And it's a created perception in our mind where Mr Blameworth keeps chattering and makes you feel incomplete or dissatisfied in life. This pushes you to do great but also keeps you dissatisfied without peace of mind and you "just can't stop it".

6. You always feel irritated, stressed, and tired because Mr Blameworth is only talking inside and keeps you busy thinking. You overthink the situation and imagine situations multiple times

It's a difficult situation, I must say, and you feel trapped in it, you don't feel like being part of the crowd but also feel alone.

Many of us name it introversion, but it is social anxiety that makes you feel troubled all the time.

I have gone through all these emotions and, it's exhausting and leaves you with no energy for no reason. 90% of the time, all your thoughts are just imaginary. We prove to others for no reason; nobody is judging you or talking bad about you, but there is a constant fear so this must be taken care of.

It's emotionally exhausting and creates a cycle of self-doubt, deeply affecting us. This fear of not being seen, understood, or visible can harm us from the inside out, creating another emotional trap to break.

And if we talk about the reasons for it, then it would be:

- Expectation of society of extroversion – our society sees extroverts as charismatic people and feels only they can be successful in life, leaving introverts feeling aloof.

  My friend Akash, a thoughtful introvert, often felt overlooked in a world that idolises extroverts. At work, louder colleagues dominated, leaving him questioning his value. But when a crucial project needed deep strategy and focus, Akash's quiet strengths shone through, leading the team to success.

  His story is proof that success isn't about being the loudest in the room—it's about bringing your unique strengths to the table.

  The pressure to perform from our childhood can be overwhelming.

  I hated it when my mom would call me over whenever Sharma uncle visited and asked about my math marks, knowing I struggled and barely passed. His constant comparison to his daughter, who excelled in math, only made it worse. These situations push us into a shell, making us reluctant to express ourselves just to impress others.

- Introverts are seen as disinterested, aloof, or anti-social. (my family called me anti-social when I am was not a part of their gossips or politics or what's up conversation, and I hated it because it's not true. Why didn't they understand that I didn't want to be part of a conversation that didn't make sense to me?

- Perception of not confident enough – sometimes quietness is mistaken as lack of confidence, but the reality is the person who talks a lot in most situations is the person who knows the least.

- Previous incidents of being ignored can also create this anxiety.

- Comparisons worsen this – comparing introverts with extroverts can create a perception of lower value and take this anxiety to the next level.

- Sometimes the desire to be visible or acknowledged can also create this anxiety.

It's important to recognise this anxiety first and then address it openly.

3. Comparison Fever: Running a race you can't win

You must have heard this before, that we should never compare ourselves to others. We don't know their stories, so our chapter 1 can be their chapter 20. Or you should always compare yourself with the person you were yesterday and blah blah blah… but still, we compare ourselves to others, and this starts from the time we are born, like this baby is fair, this baby is quite weak, you remember her baby was stronger than this baby.

I see parents stressed because their child is an inch shorter or a kilogram lighter than the neighbour's child of the same age. Even we, as parents, felt the pressure when our younger one wasn't walking while another child of the same age seemed much more active. People are strained upon 93% marks Vs 96% marks with Sharma's uncle beta, so you think we can do what we preach, I know it's difficult.

In 1954, Leon Festinger introduced a theory known as the 'Social Comparison Theory, suggesting that people evaluate their own abilities, opinions, and emotions by comparing themselves to others, and this process helps individuals gauge either upward or downward progression.

Again, let me emphasise that nothing is bad in this world if done with the right mindset and attitude, and it goes with this comparison fever too.

This is one of the subterranean pain points of life, because this comparison made me suffer a lot for a long time, impacting my self-confidence and self-esteem at a much deeper level. This was the time when Mr Blameworth dominated Mr Bliss most of the time.

Story time – I recollect this part of my life with a lot of agony, when my so-called extended family used to compare me with one of my cousins, and her name was Pooja. I was studying in an average trust school called Guru Nanak School in my hometown, Jamshedpur. The school was just like any trust government school of the 90s, where study wasn't a priority, and it was much for the degree. I remember myself bunking most of the classes and eating langar (which is the free food served by the gurudwara to all who visit daily) every other day in the nearby gurudwara. As a child, it was a normal life for me and I was just going with the flow, with the realisation that as the elder child of the family, this is the only thing I can afford at this point. During this time, my father was also struggling and trying to settle down in life while taking good care of the family and 3 young kids.

My life was similar to that of any middle-class person in the 90s, when our parents were trying to do their best to make us better people to serve society.

Now, let me take you back to my life then, when Pooja was studying in one of the best schools in Jamshedpur at that time and was quite sophisticated for the world (if not in reality). Here come my distant relatives who used to visit us almost weekly for various reasons, with one of the prime duties of comparing us with Pooja and her family.

I don't remember them talking positively about us anytime; however, they used to make us feel small. I remember my parents doing more than their capacity to keep them happy and please them to the core. I feel bad for my parents here who were under tremendous pressure to make them look good in front of our relatives without expecting any support from them.

I don't remember a single instance of them visiting us and not telling my parents how Pooja is extremely beautiful and talented unlike Julie (It's my nickname), and they can't see any hope in me doing well in life. They had a lot to say about my looks, colour, features, studies, and everything possible at that point with no hope for the future, and every time this used to break my heart, and I kept losing my confidence with time.

And I remember my mom and dad feeling inadequate and not good enough after their visit. In the last few years, I blamed my parents for being influenced and comparing me with her, but now I understand their pain and the deep pressure from family and the so-called society in showing that their kids are also good enough.

This was the time, Mr Blameworth came into existence, and from then he was unstoppable until I met Mr Bliss.

This process of comparison created a deep sense of inferiority complex and insecurity in me with a feeling of "I am not enough", and this can destroy your self-confidence and something inside you.

This habit of comparison felt like a lingering fever, unresolved for a long time—until I finally acknowledged it and took steps to heal from within

This comparison fever can create a deep sense of fear of judgement in multiple ways, such as...

- Perceived sense of lack – this comparison can create a deep sense of lack, and this lack can create a fear of being judged as inferior and less competent, along with a regular sense of anxiety about how people perceive me.

- Undue social pressure – Social comparison within the family or outside can create a sense of pressure against the so-called societal standard and expectation.

- Self-criticism – Frequent comparisons can make you your own harsh critic without realising it, and this internal critic can make you more sensitive about how people look at you, and this critic is Mr Blameworthy

- Good boy or good girl syndrome – the comparisons or judgements make you seek external validation most of the time and a persistent fear of being judged. People shouldn't see the bad side of me. This makes you behave artificially or unauthentically most of the time, and you lose your originality or uniqueness.

I am relieved that we didn't have social media in the '90s; otherwise, I would have gone mad.

Today, social media is making this issue easier to practice. Most of the time on social media, people project only a good picture, and you tend to compare your whole life to someone's small, good life, and you easily get into this trap of comparison.

Let others compare you with anyone in this world, but when you compare yourself with someone, you are making a judgement about yourself and them.

Comparison is a sin that we commit and end up killing ourselves.

Beware of this fever, which is everywhere, around you and can infect you badly. This will not only make you sick physically but will destroy your whole mental setup.

4. Friendship Fears: The Loneliness of Few

This is again a hidden issue around us, not many suffer from this, but it's quite a common one.

I have personally suffered with this a lot. I don't have many friends, and in a couple of them, I don't interact much, so you can call me a person with fewer friends.

Imagine the fear of not having many friends, where did it come from? This has come from again when we were kids and started interacting with this world, and from then, whenever anyone talks to you will ask, "do you have friends?" "how many friends do you have?" "do you have only girls or boys as friends?" – why the hell do you want to know this? What are you going to do with my personal details of my friends? Most of the time, our family members or family friends ask this question to showcase that they are our friends.

So, from childhood, we created a sense of compulsion of having many friends around, and if you do not have many friends, then you are not a social or influential person. Oh, come on, every other Sharma uncle of all the families.

When people have no or fewer friends, they can experience a sense of loneliness, which can create a fear of being judged for having no social connections. Now, when we look at it another way, having fewer friends also creates a sense of a lack of validation from the surrounding environment and increases self-doubt and anxiety about how others perceive us.

This friendship can also give rise to other issues, such as

- Social anxiety: One can feel excessively self-conscious and fearful in social situations.

- Low self-esteem: One might question their own worth or feel unlikable.

- Avoidance behaviour: Which is, again, to avoid the potential pain of being judged.

- Overcompensation: In an attempt to avoid judgement, sometimes people tend to overcompensate, which leads to personal dissatisfaction.

- Difficulty in expressing emotions – due to loneliness and the fear of judgement, sometimes people can't express their feelings well.

- Fear of rejection – the friendship fears can also create a sense of fear of rejection, which is not a natural emotion and can be harmful.

Not being part of a big group affects one's fear of judgement from those group members and doesn't allow them to live an authentic life.

Just an angle, sometimes, what seems normal to us isn't truly normal. It takes a clear view and a genuine heart to see through the things around us.

5. Social Anxiety Disorder (SAD): Drowning in Others' Expectations

I am not sure if the word SAD comes from this disorder but truly defines it.

SAD is also a phobia from society which puts you in a mental condition where you feel intense emotions with a persistent fear of being judged, embarrassed, and a feeling of humiliation, incompleteness, and insult. SAD can make a person feel disgusted all the time and make someone believe that others are constantly evaluating his/her behaviour.

Sneak Peek Time – Ritika was an incredibly talented designer, but she dreaded team presentations. Her mind raced with thoughts like, what if I stumble over my words? What if they think my ideas are stupid? Every meeting felt like standing under a harsh spotlight, with every eye judging her every move.

The fear wasn't fleeting – it consumed her. She overanalysed her tone, gestures, and even the way she sat, convinced that others were critiquing her. This persistent fear made her withdraw from team discussions and turn down opportunities that required visibility. She felt incomplete, humiliated, and disgusted with herself for not being able to push past the anxiety.

Social Anxiety Disorder (SAD) made Ritika feel trapped in a loop of fear and self-doubt, where she believed the world was always evaluating her, even when it wasn't. It wasn't until she sought help and started working on her self-perception that she began to break free from this paralysing cycle.

SAD can make you really sad in multiple ways, and let me explain that to you here, the fear of judgement where a person can feel

- Hyperaware of what others are thinking – In SAD, an individual assumes that others are judging them harshly, and the constant focus on what others think creates an intense anxiety all the time.

- Extreme fear of negative evaluation – this is one of the core features of SAD, the fear of negative evaluation.

- Hyped imagination of consequences – SAD makes you overestimate the consequences of social mistakes, e.g. - I said this to him, and now he must be thinking badly about it and might even remove me from the project. You can let your imagination spiral to the most negative scenarios possible.

- Self-criticism – people with SAD can be hard on themselves.

- Avoidance of social situations

- Physical symptoms like sweating, trembling, blushing, or a racing heart

- Stuck in a cycle of anxiety and judgement.

SAD can really make your life tough if not treated on time, however, fortunately today the world has atleast started acknowledging that there is help available to overcome these issues.

6. Choose between fire and fear: Stuck Between Dreams and Reality

The fear of judgement is one of the most common and paralysing factors for someone who is stuck between their dreams and reality. Imagine how strong this fear is, which can stop people from pursuing their passion and dreams.

Imagine the fear of rejection or being in public, which can hold you back from pursuing your vision or dreams. Let's see exactly how you feel about it.

- A feeling of fear of rejection or criticism – people often worry about how their family, friends, peers or society might react if they take a step towards their dreams. They might be criticised or questioned for their choices, so they hold back. Today, many of us want to be an entrepreneur or have a startup but don't initiate because they don't want to face criticism from their family or friends.

  Quick Sneak peek time – My husband, Kunal, has always dreamed of starting his own business. He has a brilliant idea, a solid plan, and the drive to make it happen. But every time he brings up the topic, there's a wave of apprehension from our family.

"What if it doesn't work out? How will we manage the finances?" they ask. Their concerns are valid—after all, entrepreneurship comes with uncertainties. But underneath their questions, there's an unspoken fear of stepping into the unknown, a resistance to breaking away from the comfort of a stable job.

Kunal finds himself torn. On one hand, he's passionate about his idea and feels it could be transformative—not just for him but for others, too. On the other hand, he doesn't want to upset the family or face criticism if things don't go as planned.

This hesitation isn't just about money; it's the fear of judgement. "What will people say if I leave a secure job for something so risky?" he often wonders aloud. Like so many others, he's caught between the safety of what's known and the potential of what could be.

His story is a mirror for countless aspiring entrepreneurs who dream big but hold back because they don't want to risk rejection or criticism. It's not just fear of failure—it's fear of how the world around them will perceive that failure.

- Perceived lack of support – Many of us don't pursue our dreams because we are fearful that nobody will support us, and we keep thinking "what if no one believes in me" or "what if people will make fun of me" or "what if they think I am wasting my time".

- Because we don't want to expose our flaws to all in case we fail.

- The fear of labelling or stereotyping – it's quite unfair and old-fashioned but still, people are afraid of trying something new because they don't want to be named as impractical or unrealistic.

- Fear of change – is the biggest fear of this world, the fear of how others will react to this change, and this can be a tiny change like quitting a toxic but stable job, moving to a new city or nowadays moving from an established life of a metro city back to the hometown or smaller cities or starting a new venture, etc. People often fear to be judged for bringing these changes and want to stay in a situation that feels safer or acceptable to others, even if it's unfulfilling.

I was reading an article and research from Harvard on "the biggest regret people have before they die" and the most common ones which forced me to write this book.?

One of the biggest regrets people have is that "they must have done something they loved, or they wanted to do which they didn't do over the fear of judgement."

I have missed multiple opportunities, many chances of making friends, or many moments of happiness and excitement over this dilemma and fear, so ensure to tackle it now.

Remember, Oops is always better than I wish.

7. Effort Overload: Struggling to Stay Afloat

It's a common workplace behaviour, something we often do without even realising it.

Effort overload happens when someone asks or takes on too many responsibilities just to avoid being judged negatively by others. When people are overloaded, they tend to push themselves because they fear being seen as lazy or incapable (Most common in countries like India, where there is demand supply mismatch).

Sneak Peek Time – In one of my organisation, Priya was known for her willingness to help. During meetings, she'd often volunteer to take on extra tasks, even when her workload was already heavy. It seemed like the right thing to do – being a team player, right?

One day, a colleague noticed this pattern and gently pointed out, "Priya, you always say 'yes' without even thinking about it. How are you managing everything on your plate?"

Priya was taken aback. She hadn't realised how often she agreed to take on more work, putting her own responsibilities at risk. As she reflected, she realised this unconscious habit of trying to please everyone was taking a toll on her time, energy, and mental space.

This small but common behaviour in the workplace often goes unnoticed until it starts to affect performance and well-being. Priya's realization served as a powerful reminder to all of us about the importance of setting boundaries—even when it feels difficult or uncomfortable to do so.

The overload is often out of a desire to meet others' expectations, prove their worth, and avoid disappointing people around. This constant pressure to stay afloat, juggling work, personal commitments, and societal expectations, leads to physical and mental exhaustion and a compromised family life.Sometimes the overload becomes a vicious cycle, and we overcommit because we want to prove ourselves as competent and ambitious.

The constant need to prove oneself to others, such as family, friends, boss, or society, can lead to anxiety and burnout, deepening the fear of judgement even further.

The pressure to prove can paralyse decision-making, risk-taking, and we can never think about personal growth.

The biggest problems we suffer from is "The problem of Not saying NO to people". What do you think, what is this problem? This is exactly what we are talking about. I have seen many around me who can't say NO to anyone because they keep worrying about how others will perceive them; nobody should perceive them as not a very helpful person.

Effort overload directly contributes to a constant fear of judgement because this keeps us busy.

- Avoiding judgement at all costs – imagine the intensity of fear that we are ready to work and die at any cost but don't want to be judged; this is too much.

Another name for perfectionism could be an image makeover for some people 😊

Ultimately, overcoming effort overload and a constant fear of judgement is vital if you want to live a real, authentic, and fulfilling life.

8. Dream Dilemma: Judged by Our Aspirations

Story time – I am from a place called Nalanda, a small district in Bihar, known as the home of the world's first residential university, which was once an epitome of knowledge and learning until it was destroyed by Bakhtiyar Khilji. I grew up living with my grandparents and started my education in a nearby government school. During this time, my father was striving to establish himself in Jamshedpur, a city bustling with competition and ambitious individuals.

Around the age of 7, I moved to Jamshedpur. It was a new place for me, and we lived a simple life typical of the '90s, staying in a small rented one-bedroom flat. Despite the challenges, hats off to my mother, who managed everything so gracefully. The space was tiny, but she kept the house running smoothly with 3 kids, 2 adults, and a frequent stream of visitors. Her ability to handle it all with such poise was truly admirable.

Somehow, I believe life was tougher back then, yet people seemed happier. We cherished every small moment of joy, success, or celebration without overanalysing it

So, when I started my life in such a humble way, it was difficult for me to dream big. And I remember my mother saying, "Beta, you shouldn't dream bigger than your status."

But (with a capital B), I always dreamed BIG. I was always curious to know what stops us from seeing bigger dreams and why we should dream small.

I remember people kept judging us for everything and on what we wanted to do or be in life, but still, I dreamed and visualised big.

I was a student of Hindi medium from the state board but wanted to study in the best school, which couldn't happen. I wanted to be a doctor but that also couldn't happen. I cleared some entrance exam of Private medical colleges, but the course fee was beyond our reach. So, I kept thinking big and convinced my family to send me to a bigger place for studies. My parents supported me, and since then, I never looked back and never stopped dreaming big.

People used to judge me on my looks, skills, and status, but somewhere, I was shouting inside of me, "Why are you judging me on what I was, or I am now? Judge me on my dreams and where I want to be," and what's wrong in that.

I remember once someone from my extended family visited us and, as usual, asked my mom, "What do you think about Julie (my nickname)?" My mom replied, "She wants to be a doctor." The visitor immediately responded without giving it a thought, "But why? Graduation is enough for her. It's high time you started looking for a boy to get her married soon, and in spite of all the advancement in India parents still want their daughters to get married early.

So, one thing is for sure, that society cannot digest your dreams which they can't visualise, and this also guarantees that you shouldn't be bothered about them.

You can become and achieve what you can dream, but the dream dilemma is real and haunting for many.

Dream dilemma is a real struggle people face when they want to chase their dreams but are worried about how others will judge them for those dreams. And it's a conflict between what you really want and dealing with other people's opinions about it.

Another story time - In 2015, I was in Bangalore and had the opportunity to interview with a prestigious multinational company. It was an exciting process, and after clearing six rigorous rounds, I found myself in the final HR round, feeling confident and hopeful.

As I sat across from the HR head, the conversation seemed to be going well. Then came the question that caught me off guard: "What do you want to be in life?"

Without a second thought, I replied honestly, "I want to be the youngest CEO in this industry without owning the organization." My intent was clear—I wanted to achieve this through hard work, dedication, and exceptional results.

But the reaction was unexpected. The HR head looked at me with a mix of disbelief and skepticism. Later, I was informed that I had been rejected. The feedback stung: "She is either out of her mind or too aggressive for this role."

That moment taught me a valuable lesson about perception and the importance of framing ambition in a way that resonates with others. While I stood by my aspirations, I realized that being misunderstood can sometimes be part of the journey toward achieving big dreams.

So, the real judgement happens, and people judge you critically on your dreams. Or maybe we can say, "An average or ordinary person can't digest an extraordinary dream which is out of their eyesight, so they start criticising you for that."

We avoid seeing bigger dreams like launching our own start-up or doing something unconventional like studying art forms or trying something new like making a career as a social media influencer because society can't digest it and starts judging you harshly.

I met someone in Mumbai, a young girl who wanted to be a criminologist, but her parents didn't allow, quoting "what will people say" (log kya kahenge), "can't you choose something prestigious like becoming a doctor or engineer or an IAS.

Imagine situations like perusing an unconventional career like a tech startup, choosing a non-traditional path like travelling the world on a caravan, venturing into a new hobby like gaming, breaking away from social norms like homeschooling, making a major life-changing decision like leaving a job for a social cause, taking a stand on a controversial issue like social justice, etc. Can you deal with these situations without a fear of judgement?

Ask a few questions to ourselves now and think if this really makes sense.

- Am I holding back from pursuing my dream because I'm afraid of what others will think?

- What is the priority for me: others' opinion or my life?

- What's the worst that could happen if I followed my aspirations, regardless of judgement?

- Am I avoiding certain topics or goals during conversations to evade criticism or the fear of judgement?

- How would my life look if I stopped worrying about being judged?

- What are the core values driving my dreams, and why do they matter to me?

- Am I giving up or altering my dreams to fit societal expectations or norms?

Ask these questions and think if what others think is more important than your own life.

The "Dream Dilemma" is the struggle people face when they want to chase their dreams but are worried about others' judgement.

Essentially, it is the conflict between what you really want and dealing with others' opinions about it.

So, it's very clear that dream dilemma happens when your personal aspirations are met with the fear of judgement, and this fear can hold you back from pursuing your true dreams and goals.

And the last question I want you to keep thinking about is, "Why become normal, when you can become the best?"

9. Family Frustrations: Balancing Tradition and Modernity

This is again an exceptionally common challenge we see around, which fuels the real fear of judgement.

With family frustrations, I mean the challenges and stress that arise when individuals or families try to balance the traditional values with the practices of modern way of life.

This is normally experienced with middle-class families, particularly where generational and cultural differences lead to conflicts about lifestyle choices, beliefs, and expectations.

And in this friction, we see the 2 opposing forces, especially in the fast-changing world of the younger generation where the priority is individualism, freedom, and new ways of thinking, while the older generation may value duty, respect for tradition, and communal values.

We often face this fear of judgement during major life decisions influenced by what others might say.

- Career choices – this is quite common nowadays when parents may expect their children to follow some stable, prestigious career like medicine, law or family businesses. If you ask the reason for it, they will mention financial security and for the societal respect. So, the motto is driven by society for society.

  At the same time, the young generation may seek non-traditional careers in creative fields, startups, or entrepreneurship, which could be seen as risky or unconventional.

  Here, the clash between security and passion may lead to disappointment or judgement from family or society.

- Marriage and relationships – again a common one where you shouldn't marry someone you love but someone from the same community because of the same reason: "what people will say". So again, a dangerous judgement trap where we feel forced to either sacrifice our own happiness to maintain family harmony.

This has happened to me, and I feel it when the whole society was against our relationship and marriage because my husband and I were from different communities, but I am happy that these judgements are fading away a bit.

- Housewife vs. Househusband role - there are many issues like gender roles, where a woman can be a housewife, but a man cannot be a househusband because society can't accept it well For centuries, husbands have been seen as the primary breadwinners, and this long-standing tradition is now being challenged

There are many other issues which we see around us like lifestyle choices, parenting style with old school discipline vs modern approaches, technology and communications as modern connectivity vs tradition etc.

And you know how this clash within the family and within society creates the fear of judgement or the Judgement trap

- Conflicting values and the extreme fear of rejection – The basic emotions we have with our family are the sense of belongingness. When our values differ from those of our families, we start losing this sense of connection and feel trapped between being true to ourselves or doing what we want versus seeking family approval. Many a times you will see that the family starts falling apart due to this conflicting values. The older generation will have to let go of some values of the past and the newer generation needs to find a middle ground for a healthier family dynamic.

- Risk of emotional isolation – Normally people avoid these clashes with family or people they love because this makes them emotionally isolated, and they start feeling trapped in harsh criticism or exclusion.

- Internalised judgement – Over time people start to internalise family judgements which create self-doubt and a sense of guilt, and this paralyses them into the judgement trap, where they can't move forward with their dreams or live authentically without fearing family disapproval.

- The Weight of Expectations – Family expectations, especially rooted during childhood and a long-standing tradition, carry significant weight. The fear of not living up to these expectations can make people in need of constant external validation. In this condition, people feel they must sacrifice their personal happiness and growth to avoid this judgement.

So, never take the judgement trap lightly because this can make you sacrifice everything you love, and you need to live an authentic life.

However, we are not even aware if we are in this trap. Let me ask you a few questions, and then you decide if you are already a part of this trap or not.

- Why do I feel the need to dress around my family or specific people, even if it's not how I want to dress?

- Are you always worried about how people will judge you based on your appearance, like clothes, hairstyle, or makeup?

- Are you afraid to post something on social media because you fear being judged by family or friends?

- Is your current job due to family pressure, or do you really enjoy your work?

- Are you trying to be fit to fit into societal standards, or are you doing it for your own health and happiness?

- Are you pressured to keep in touch with some people and not to be in touch with others because your family expects it?

- Do you avoid expressing your true opinions or thoughts on political, religious, or lifestyle choices because you are afraid of being judged?

- Are you making financial decisions to impress people or show off?

Ask yourself these questions repeatedly. If most of your answers are negative, it indicates that you are caught in the trap. Otherwise, you are among the lucky few who live as their true selves.

The fear of judgement can influence your actions, words, or decisions. Being aware of these instances helps you identify where the judgement trap is at work in your daily life and gives you the opportunity to break free and live truer to yourself.

10. Cultural variances: Fear of Judgement in a Diverse World

Sometimes cultural differences, value systems, and norms can shape the fear of judgement in an individual.

In our ever more connected world, cultural differences significantly impact our experiences and perceptions. Various cultures possess unique values, norms, and expectations that shape how individuals view themselves and those around them.

The cultural variances create a daily, real-life challenge for many who are trying to navigate multiple cultural systems and often feel judged in the path they choose.

Here, when we talk about cultural variances, we are not only talking about people from different countries but also people within the same country, city, and community with completely different value systems and traditions.

It also highlights internal conflict that arises when different cultural expectations come into play, leading to the fear of judgement.

In India, you don't need to travel to other countries to experience this feeling. I have experienced it closely.

I am from East India but have spent most of my time in South and West India with completely different cultural norms and expectations. I remember when I left my hometown, Jamshedpur, and landed in Vizag, it was a different world for me.

People judged me for my language, my accent, looks, and overall existence, so it's obvious that culture plays a critical role in creating this fear of judgement.

When you move from one state to another , like I moved from the eastern state of Jharkhand to the southern state of Telangana, everything changes.

When you change a place, there is a difference in:

- Tradition
- Belief system
- Language
- Different perceptions on wealth and education
- New social circles
- Different communal expectations
- Cultural identity

And this change brings a lot of new perceptions and circumstances which are new to you and create a fear of judgement or fear of unknown.

To avoid the fear of judgement in such a situation, you can adopt these strategies.

- **Understand Triggers**: Identify why you feel judged and address it calmly.

- **Practice Self-Compassion**: Remind yourself that it's okay to feel out of place initially. Everyone has been a newcomer at some point.

- **Embrace Curiosity**: View cultural differences as opportunities to learn.

- **Foster Connections**: Focus on shared values and build rapport through conversations.

- **Start Small**: Interact in less intimidating settings to build confidence.

- **Reframe Thoughts**: Remind yourself that most people are not judging you.

- **Celebrate Wins**: Acknowledge even small steps outside your comfort zone.

- **Promote Inclusivity**: Encourage openness and celebrate diversity.

And please keep your cheerleader Mr. Bliss with you all the time.

While cultural differences can intensify the fear of judgement, they also offer opportunities for connection and growth.

By sharing our experiences and learning from one another, we can foster a sense of belonging that goes beyond cultural boundaries.

Navigating the fear of judgement in a diverse world requires awareness and openness. By recognising the role of cultural variances, we can cultivate a more inclusive environment that embraces individuality while celebrating our shared humanity.

11. The Trap of Overgeneralising: How One Mistake/Thought Can Shape Our Fear

Have you ever felt like one mistake makes you a failure? Or did you ever tell yourself, "I always mess up" or "I can't get anything right" or "Am I good or even deserve this"?

There are situations that can arise from job rejection, social slip-ups, breakups, or if you are struggling with a project or even parenting mistakes. We tend to overgeneralise things and create a negative cycle that fuels fear and self-doubt.

This has happened to me multiple times but let me share my journey with you. There were moments when overgeneralising really troubled my state of mind.

Sneak Peek Time – In the early years of motherhood, I found myself grappling with an overwhelming sense of guilt and inadequacy. My elder daughter lived with my in-laws while my husband and I navigated our demanding jobs and daily chores in bustling Mumbai.

As I rushed through each day, the constant thought that I was failing as a mother haunted me.

I believed that by not having her with me, I was somehow neglecting my duties and failing to provide the nurturing environment she deserved, and it may affect our mother-daughter bond.

Every time I heard a well-meaning friend or family member suggest that I should be with my child, it intensified my feelings of inadequacy.

I remember people judging me and saying, "How can you keep your kid away from you?" and this judgemental thought made Mr. Blameworth (my inner critic) quite rude to me.

I started overgeneralising my situation, thinking that if I wasn't physically present with her every moment, I must be a "bad mother." This mindset created a cycle of self-doubt that loomed over me, leading to unnecessary stress and anxiety.

However, everything changed when we welcomed our second daughter into our lives. This time, I decided to keep her with us full time. To my surprise, I soon realised that my first daughter had thrived in her time with her grandparents. They provided her with love, wisdom, and experiences that enriched her development in ways I hadn't fully appreciated before. Our bond remained intact, and she flourished under their care And my relationship with my in-laws also grew stronger, as they had always wanted my elder daughter to stay with them. They came to understand that I had sacrificed my experience of motherhood for their sake.

Through this experience, I learned a valuable lesson about the dangers of overgeneralising. I had let a single narrative shape my fear of judgement, both from others and myself. My initial thoughts about being a bad mother were not only unfounded, but they also distracted me from appreciating the love and support my family was providing.

This journey taught me that one wrong thought can distort our reality and foster a fear of judgement that isn't based on facts.

It's essential to recognise that every situation is unique and that we should embrace our individual paths without succumbing to societal pressures or internalised judgements. By acknowledging the positive aspects of our circumstances, we can break free from the trap of overgeneralisation and allow ourselves to thrive.

Overgeneralisation can create a convincing trap that feeds our fear of judgement, limiting our growth and potential.

Understanding Overgeneralisation

Overgeneralisation occurs when we draw broad conclusions based on a single incident.

Let's visualise a scenario, if you receive criticism for a presentation, you might think, "I always mess up," or "I'm terrible at public speaking." This type of thinking creates a cycle of self-doubt and reinforces the fear of being judged by others.

The Consequences of Overgeneralisation

Overgeneralisation can make us:

- Feel anxious in situations that remind us of our past failures and we get trapped in the fear of making the same mistakes.

- Self-limiting beliefs – this makes us feel like a loser, making us believe that we can't succeed

- Damaged relationships – Overgeneralisation can affect our relationships, fearing that others will judge us based on past experiences, leading to isolation and loneliness.

How to Fight Overgeneralisation

This is a daunting feeling to deal with because it can create a strong sense of fear of judgement and make you feel afraid in any situation.

And the simple way to deal with it is,

- Always challenge negative thoughts – challenge your negative thoughts with facts or feelings and try to provide multiple instances of how they are not true

- Focus on details and don't ever generalise stuff – instead of generalising anything, try to focus on specifics of what went wrong and how it can be improved.

- Celebrate small wins - Acknowledge your achievements, no matter how small. By celebrating each step forward, you reinforce a positive self-image that helps combat the tendency to overgeneralise.

- Seek support – and this is important to share your fears and bad experiences with your supporters, friends, or mentors so that they can show you ways to deal with it.

Overgeneralisation can be a significant trap that amplifies our fear of judgement, hindering our growth and potential.

By identifying this cognitive distortion and applying strategies to combat it, we can liberate ourselves from the constraints of fear and pursue a more genuine, fulfilling life.

Keep in mind that one setback doesn't define you; it's just a stepping stone on your journey to success.

12. English confidence struggle – seriously?

I must say this is one of the most common causes of low self-confidence and a prominent reason for the fear of being judged as not intelligent simply because you don't know English. It's strange, but unfortunately, it's true in India.

India is the second-largest English-speaking country after the USA with almost 135 million people, which is about 10% of the population. So, if you see 1 out of 10 Indian adults can speak English.

Source   (https://www.shapernet.in/2021/03/india-holds-largest-english-speaking.html)

Now, India has over 121 languages and 270 mother tongues, making it one of the most linguistically diverse countries in the world. The Indian government recognises 22 official languages, including Hindi and English, and India is the only country where there is a frequent switch between one language and another in daily conversation. For example, if you visit Maharashtra, you need to switch between English and Marathi; if you visit Andhra Pradesh or Telangana, you need to switch between English and Telugu. This is the case with almost all the states and Union territories.

This makes India one of the most language-diverse countries, and fluency can be an issue for many.

Another reason is that people from non-English medium schools may not have fluent language skills because they have studied in another language, which is absolutely fine.

Knowing English is an advantage, but this doesn't make you superior or smart. It's just a language.

Here, the main problem is that people view English as more than just a language – but as a mark of intelligence, success, and social status. (I know it sounds a bit pitiful, but let's be real, folks – it's the truth)

When an Englishman can't speak our local language, it's obvious, but when being an Indian you can't speak a foreign language, then why are you being judged on it.

Some questions we should ask ourselves.

Why do people in India often think you're smart or successful only if you speak good English? Does this make us forget the value of our own languages?

And there are people who can talk fluently in English, but they don't have the basic IQ to qualify as an intellect. They are getting jobs easily, and many skillful people are struggling with low confidence because their English is not so good. BUT WHY?

Why do people feel embarrassed or judged in India if they don't speak English well?

Does using so much English in daily life make us lose touch with our culture and local languages?

Is not knowing English really a barrier to success in India, or are there other ways to be successful without it?

People who are not fluent in English often face judgement or feel inferior in environments where English proficiency is highly rated, especially in places like workplaces, schools, and social gatherings.

Story time - Let me share my story. I began my education at a government school there, and when I was about 10 years old, we moved to Jamshedpur. Despite my age, I had grasped the basics well enough to be admitted directly into the 3rd standard, skipping the earlier grades. The school I attended was quite basic, or perhaps below average, with minimal fees, which is where I started my primary schooling.

I continued my education in Hindi medium until the 10th standard. Back then, , and the government didn't emphasise English as a core subject. Instead, Sanskrit was compulsory for us.

Up until my 10th standard, I had never studied in English. It was a completely foreign language to me, and I had zero proficiency in it. After completing my 12th, where I studied science in English, I was introduced to the language but with very minimal proficiency. I then moved to Vishakhapatnam for my graduation in Biotechnology, where most people were quite fluent in English.

My initial days there were daunting. I couldn't understand the language others were speaking, and I struggled to communicate. Because of my poor English skills, I often isolated myself and avoided conversations, lacking confidence. Some even made fun of me, which made me extremely self-conscious.

This was the time I started learning English. I faced all the challenges that come with learning a new language, and it had a significant impact on my self-image and confidence.

Today, I am quite proficient and comfortable in English, and I even work as a communications professional in a Forbes top 100 company with their Head Quarters in Germany.

This journey shows that English is just a language – it doesn't define who you are or your worth.

I remember the struggle of knowing nothing to reaching a comfortable stage and how it was complicatedly linked to self-judgement. It was not only the fear of how others would perceive me and think about me, but also that I was harsh on myself.

I suffered from self-judgement, and it was rough and awful; it was a lot...

- Feeling of inadequacy – I considered myself a failure and was suffering from the wrong notion that if I don't know English, then I can't succeed.

- Negative self-talk – I was engaged in a lot of negative self-talk where I thought, "How can I learn English now? It's too late," and "I'll never be good enough," or "I shouldn't even try." I had many unwanted thoughts that kept me disturbed and suffered from low self-esteem.

- A cycle of self-doubt – because I wasn't good enough, I avoided participating or communicating, which further damaged my self-confidence.

- Impact on growth – this self-judgement suppresses personal growth. I never wanted to do anything because I believed that I would definitely fail.

- Comparison to others – In a group setting, I always used to think, "I wish I was fluent like others," and this comparison fuelled self-judgement and kept me in pain at that point in time.

When I realised this connection between English confidence struggle and self-judgement, I started to shift my mindset because that's the way it works.

And now I comprehend the fact that English fluency shouldn't be a reason to judge someone or feel low on confidence. Like me, you need to understand language is just a tool to communicate, not a measure of your worth or potential, and here is why:

- Your skills and personality matter more – what you know is more important than how you speak, and there are millions of successful people who have made it big without being fluent in English, which is just a language.

- You are more than a language – Confidence comes from who you are, and not from how well you can speak a foreign language. Your value as a person is based on your character, your hard work, and your kindness—not your English fluency.

- Every language has value. One language, according to some, is more important than another merely because it is popularly viewed. Besides, the language that you are best acquainted with has its respective beauty and depths, and knowing it well amounts to just another feat at a personal level. Today, many developed countries, such as China and Azerbaijan, have thriving economies and flourishing societies, despite a significant portion of their populations not knowing basic English.

- Fluency comes with practice - It's okay that you're struggling in English; it doesn't mean you'll never improve. Like a skill, it takes time and effort, while being in a learning process shouldn't discourage your confidence. For instance – Once we had an Uzbek singer who flawlessly performed all the Bollywood songs, even though she didn't know a single word of Hindi. She practiced for just 3-4 days and absolutely rocked the event!

- People care about connections, not perfections - An English-speaking person simply wants to understand you. It really doesn't matter if your English isn't perfect; what matters are your ideas, thoughts, and feelings.

- To be successful does not require language fluency. In the world, thousands of people become extraordinary entrepreneurs, creating good works without speaking perfect English. Your fast confidence will take you to places that may otherwise seem impossible through the limitation of language.

Never judge or be judged by someone's broken English; this means they know another language better than you.

And never get offended easily if someone makes fun of your English; it's just a foreign language, like German or French, with the difference that it has become a global language now and is used widely, nothing more than that.

13. Inferiority Complex: Rude Self-Judgement for No Reasons

You walk into a room full of people, and suddenly, a wave of self-doubt hits you hard. Everyone seems so confident, effortlessly engaging in conversations while you stand there, feeling like an outsider. You've got ideas to share, but you stay silent, convinced that what you say won't matter. As you watch others speak, you begin to think they're smarter, more successful, and somehow more deserving of being there.

You rehearse sentences in your head, afraid that one wrong word will expose you as inadequate. You catch yourself comparing your journey to theirs, wondering if you'll ever measure up. Even though you have dreams and goals, you hesitate to share them because deep down, you fear that someone else could do it better.

After the event, you replay every interaction in your mind, over-analysing every word, worrying that you've made a fool of yourself.

Have you ever wondered why we let that little voice in our head stop us from being ourselves or allow us to feel inferior?

Here's the truth: No one was actually judging you. It was your own inner critic that convinced you otherwise.

It was your own inferiority complex or rude self-judgement for no reason, and you are not alone.

Let me share one of the many times I dealt with rude self-judgement in my journey.

Story time – I remember one of the incidents from the initial days of my job. This was my second organisation as a Product Manager where I was managing my pharmaceutical brands. It was my first brainstorming session or meeting with the top management with about 20 to 25 people, including the heads of marketing, sales, purchase, legal, R&D, strategy, including the managing director, on how to maximise the sales and profit for the brands in the organisation. As the brand owner, I was expected to present my ideas. I had never attended such high-level meetings before.

I remember the stress building up the moment I heard about the meeting.

The day finally arrived. I had a thousand butterflies in my stomach and felt completely out of place. As I entered the room, filled with self-doubt and low confidence, I kept thinking about how everyone else seemed so confident and relaxed, with something valuable to add. I wondered what I could contribute and if my ideas would even make sense. I was convinced people would laugh at my thoughts, so I decided to stay quiet and avoid engaging.

When my turn came to share my idea, I was able to escape presenting because my brand was doing reasonably well. But at the end of the five-hour meeting, the managing director asked if I wanted to add anything. I had an idea the entire time and knew it could work, but I didn't have the courage to speak up. Instead, I shared it with the Product Manager sitting beside me, as that was all the confidence I could gather.

She immediately presented my idea, and to my surprise, it was considered the best idea of the day. Everyone applauded her creativity.

She enjoyed the recognition and reward for her confidence, while I silently regretted letting self-judgement hold me back.

The incident left me shaken, and I realised that it was no one but me who was judgemental. I was being very harsh on myself for no reason.

During that time, Mr Blameworth was my closest companion, and I spent most of my days with him. However, immediately after that incident, I began to hear the voice of Mr Bliss within me, which led me to connect more deeply with him instead.

This happens to many of us, and you must have also experienced it at some point in your life.

Inferiority complex can be felt as a feeling of inadequacy, "I am not enough," and everyone is continuously evaluating and criticising me.

Sometimes it's good because it motivates you to improve, but if this feeling stays longer it can have a negative impact.

Inferiority complex can deeply affect the fear of being judged, even when there is no real external danger.

It's ironic that what we often perceive as judgement from others is really just self-judgement. In reality, no one is judging us. Self-judgement is internal, real, and far more daunting than any external criticism.

Today, inferiority complex is a bigger problem than it looks on the surface. This is an unexpressed emotion which makes people suffer silently.

Common driving factors which we should be careful of today are as follows:

- Social media comparison – which is useless and over-idealised.

- Unrealistic standard of success – which is extremely exaggerated.

- Early life experiences – which are mostly driven by wrong comparisons.

- Career pressure – again with undue competitive culture, killing authenticity.

- Body image issue – thanks to the modern beauty industry.

- Lack of validation – something you must ignore.

- Perfectionism – which is, again, very overhyped and a total waste of time

The toughest critic we encounter isn't the outside world—it's the voice within us.

An inferiority complex acts like a funhouse mirror, distorting our view and amplifying our fears and doubts. We confine ourselves to self-criticism, convinced we're not good enough, while everyone else appears so self-assured and secure. However, the truth is, it's not others who hinder us—it's our own relentless inner critic.

When we cease to compare ourselves to others and release the notion that we're somehow "less than," we begin to uncover the vast potential we possess.

The anxiety of being judged often mirrors the severity with which we judge ourselves.

True liberation starts when we recognise that our worth isn't defined by comparison. More often than not, the storms of doubt we experience are ones we invoke ourselves—even when there's no storm present at all.

14. Impostor Syndrome: The Confidence Gap

Am I really good enough?

Did I just get lucky?

What if people find out I am not so talented?

Do I deserve this promotion or recognition?

Why do people think I am worthy?

Am I about to fail?

I am not as talented as people think.

Why am I not as smart as my peers?

Do I belong here?

Shouldn't I know more by now?

If I ask for help, will people realise I don't know enough?

Have you ever questioned yourself with these thoughts? Have you ever felt miserable with these thoughts? If yes, don't worry, you are not alone.

About 25 to 30% of high achievers may suffer from this condition called "Imposter syndrome," and around 70% of adults may experience it once in their lifetime.

Imposter syndrome is a behavioural health phenomenon where you can see self-doubt of intellect, skills, or accomplishments among high-achieving individuals.

It's a feeling of not being worthy of your success, despite evidence that you are. I know it's peculiar but quite common in intelligent people.

I have come across many highly confident fools and individuals with a sense of low self-worth and intellect, and it's a universal issue.

Sneak Peek Time – I have experienced it multiple times. I am not claiming that I am a higher achiever, but this has happened to me recently when I got into the global role in my current organisation.

Coming from such a humble background, first of all, I never imagined myself being in a Fortune 100 global organisation, and nobody from my family, not even my husband, thought this was possible.

And when I got into this organisation, I kept thinking, do I deserve this, or did I just get lucky? And when I got into the global role after multiple interviews and rejections, again I was asking the same question: "Do I deserve this or did I get lucky?"

And at this point I always remember two of my mentors, Subroto Banerjee and Koustubh Kanade, who always believed in me and taught me to dream big.

So, it happens. People experience this often once they achieve something, that they got lucky, and others may think that I don't belong here.

The feeling can happen to anyone, but mostly this happens with those who are genuinely talented or successful.

Anyone can feel this in scenarios like:

- In Universities – mostly after getting the scholarship, many may feel that they don't deserve their success, and their intelligence is not enough to sustain.
- In Social Situations – maybe at high-status parties, you may feel out of place.

- At Work – in leadership positions, you may feel you don't deserve this promotion and only got lucky.

- When taking on a challenge – with doubt if you are truly capable of handling it.

- When you don't have all the answers – and you feel like you should know more and asking for help might feel like you are not competent enough

But when do you feel this way?

When you compare yourself to others, you feel so

When you evaluate your accomplishments through the opinions of others, you feel so

When you try to fit in and stand out in a place where you don't belong, you feel so

So, when we see ourselves always in the mirror of others and with others' perception, we feel so.

By the way, according to experts, Imposter syndrome is of 5 common types, like:

- **The Perfectionist**: Believes that everything must be done perfectly. If they make even a small mistake, they feel like a failure and doubt their abilities.

- **The Superhuman**: Feels like they must work harder than everyone else to prove their worth. They push themselves to take on too much, believing they need to be the best at everything.

- **The Natural Genius**: Thinks they should be able to succeed easily or on the first try. If something is difficult or takes time to learn, they feel inadequate.

- **The Soloist**: Believes they must accomplish things on their own. They avoid asking for help because they think doing so will reveal their "incompetence."

- **The Expert**: Feels they need to know everything before starting something. They worry they don't know enough and are constantly seeking more knowledge to feel competent.

Some people experience imposter syndrome due to a combination of personal, social, or adjoining factors like:

- Upbringing – this is one of the basic and major reasons for imposter syndrome, putting a lot of pressure on children can make them feel like imposters later in life.

- Very high personal standard – normally seen by perfectionists.

- Fear of failure – a deep fear of failure leads to the feeling of self-doubt.

- Comparison to others – constant and unfair comparison leads to the feeling of self-pity or inaccuracy.

- External validation – if someone is driven by external validation, then people can question their own worth.

- Biases – basic social biases also suggest that some people don't belong in some spaces

And from another perspective, we suffer with this imposter is a close connection with your Mr Blameworth.

When your Mr Blameworth keeps talking in a language like:

- You are fat.

- You are not good enough.

- You do not fit in.

- You are not beautiful.

- You are below average, etc.

These statements will come from Mr Blameworth on any normal day, which is far from the truth, or an illusion, and people feel like imposters.

Anyone can feel like an imposter in this situation, so again, keep your friend Mr Bliss with you for your safety.

And remember,

When you truly become who you are, you'll live authentically, and when you are being your real self, it's impossible to become an imposter.

Part 3

Let's Demol`ish the
Boundaries of Judgement

Chapter 6

Armer Up – Start by Acknowledging It First as First Step To Mastering Judgement

Every change starts with you, and you can't expect to change things that you can't change for yourself, so let's start with a small step today.

The greatest barrier to embracing authenticity is, of course, the fear of judgement, as we discussed in detail already.

Often enough, we find ourselves paralysed by what others would say.

As a result, we halt our true self.

Knowing that fear is the first step to avoid running from it rather than away from it, in this chapter, let us discuss how a person can break free from these shackles of judgement by society after being strong enough to own those fears.

Judgement is bound to happen - It's overwhelming when it comes from the outside, from peers or family, or by societal expectations. Or sometimes it comes from our own internal critics.

The way to cut off is to confront them. When we acknowledge our fears, we step boldly into reclaiming our lives.

The Power of Acknowledgement

When I experienced it - I began experiencing this back in Bangalore. After facing several rejections, I realised that I needed to acknowledge my disappointment and not let it affect my self-esteem. Instead of torturing myself by suppressing my emotions or letting them define me, I decided to take a step back and reflect on what had happened."

I realised that it did not implicate my vision; it merely meant the opportunity was not on the same planet as the one I needed to pursue. This acceptance was important – it helped me process my emotions and understand that rejection is just a part of the growth.

How it was so transforming - Understanding my emotions helped me regain confidence and clarity. It led me to pursue other opportunities and, ultimately, to move from Bangalore to Mumbai. This brought new experiences, connections, and a sense of purpose I had not expected. Perhaps I would never have taken a chance or stepped out of my comfort zone if I had gotten that job.

The key takeaway from my story - This experience taught me the profound impact of acceptance. By engaging with my feelings of rejection and understanding their role in my journey, what initially seemed like a dead-end became an opportunity for growth. It reinforced the idea that acceptance is the first and most powerful step towards using judgement and setbacks to propel ourselves towards our true potential. After this, rejections and failures no longer daunted me as they once did.

Acknowledgement of your fear of judgement finally brings light to the shadows that haunt you. Everyone should understand this: nobody has been judged without judgement first happening against them.

When you realise you are not alone in this struggle, then you can start breaking down the barriers that keep you from being yourself.

The journey of Armer Up is not about eliminating fear; it's about acknowledging it and taking control of your narrative.

By recognising your fears, you pave the way for authentic self-expression.

Remember, judgement is often a reflection of others' insecurities, not your worth.

As you learn to Armour Up, you'll find the courage to break free from the confines of judgement and embrace the incredible person you are meant to be.

Sometimes, we shouldn't judge the judgement and understand it as a force of action that shapes your reaction.

Acknowledgement is the first step in transforming the fear of judgement from a paralysing force into a powerful catalyst for personal growth.

Here is why recognising and owning your fears is crucial:

- This helps break the cycle of shame or self-doubt.
- Helps empower self-reflection.
- Provides a sense of control.
- Strengthen your authenticity.
- Helps use judgement as a tool for growth.
- Building strength.
- Helps connect with people with the right mindset.

The power of self-acknowledgement is transformative.

It serves as the foundation for handling judgement effectively, allowing you to turn fear into fuel for growth.

By recognising and owning your feelings, you not only free yourself from the shackles of judgement but also embrace your authentic self.

As you navigate the complexities of judgement, remember that acknowledgement is not the end of the journey – it's the courageous first step towards a more empowered and fulfilling life.

Chapter 7

Understand Who's Judging and Why - Only the Stuck Stand in Judgement

Do we judge?

Why do we judge?

What does my judgement of others say about me?

How does this judgement affect me?

What makes me judge others or what makes others judge others?

How would I feel if I were judged the same way?

What makes me judgemental, fear or seeking validation?

How can I turn judgement into curiosity?

I think the time has come to reflect on the deeper questions like this, which can address the elephant in the room and explain the basics of judgement.

Before we jump into the discussion of who and why, let's consider some thought-provoking facts about judgement:

- We judge someone before we even realise it – we make our judgement in just 0.1 seconds. Research shows that humans make a first impression within a tenth of a second based on someone's appearance, expressions, and body language.

- Judgement is mostly based on incomplete information – Research proves that humans make judgements mostly with limited or biased information.

- We judge ourselves more harshly than we judge others – studies have proven that self-judgement is harsher than judging someone else.

- Judgement is nothing but a self-reflection – Psychologically, we often judge others as a defence mechanism to avoid confronting our own insecurities or flaws. So, it's a simple way to distract ourselves from dealing with our issues.

- The more you judge, the less empathetic you are as a person – research suggests that judgement activates our brain's "Default mode network" where we focus on judgement more than giving our thoughts, and it reduces our ability to think, understand, feel, and empathise. So, "Thinking is difficult so mostly people judge."

- Judgement gives you a false sense of power – research also suggests that judgement gives people a temporary and false sense of superiority or control or power. This sense of power is quite momentary and makes you feel unpleasant afterward.

You can see here research and studies which indicate how judgement is deeply ingrained in human psychology and how it impacts us.

But wait, do you know that we as humans can be quite creative and funny when it comes to judgement, and we have the talent to judge people on any random things.

We judge people on:

- Their email addresses.

- On their shopping carts.

- How someone handles their phone and takes a selfie.

- From their pet names.

- From the movies or songs they like

- What kind of emojis do people use?

- Their Starbucks order, food choices... and the list can go on.

In fact, sometimes we judge people on things we do too, like "Look at them wasting their time and life on social media. Oh, wait, let me just check this notification now😊 😊

Hence, one thing for sure is that judgement is like the brain in hibernation and so we love it.

We have already discussed the anatomy and psychology behind judgement before, now let's try to understand who is judging you all the time? Who is it that you are afraid of judgement? Who is making your life tough with random judgements? Who is not allowing you to live your true life?

Let's talk about the people who think it's their job to judge others. You see them everywhere, and they help create the fear of judgement in our society. These folks are the real villains of society, and it's important to know why you shouldn't let their opinions affect you.

And here we are:

a. **Self-created Fashion Critics** – This group will always judge you on your appearance, external beauty, or superficial qualities.

They believe their views dictate what's stylish or acceptable in society, which isn't true, but who would tell them.

You shouldn't bother about them because their judgement is often shallow and constantly changing. What's good today will be outdated tomorrow, and this doesn't define your true worth.

Mini Moment here - At one of my cousin's weddings, I wore a simple, traditional dress that I loved. But many around me, self-proclaimed fashion critics, judged me for not wearing a trendy designer outfit. It reminded me how superficial such judgements can be and how they don't define our true worth.

b. **Self-appointed Moral Monitors** – They are self-appointed and acclaimed moral inspectors and for them, everyone is bad who doesn't adhere to their belief system. And why you shouldn't care about them, because ethics vary from person to person, and you have the right to live by your own principles.

Just a swift snap - At a corporate event, while most of my colleagues were enjoying drinks, I decided to stick to soft drinks. Some of them remarked that I was being "too rigid" or "missing out on the fun."

I reminded myself that my personal choices don't need to align with others' expectations. I have the right to live by my own values, regardless of their judgements.

c. **Self-acclaimed experts** – This is quite a common group of people you can see around you, and they are "I know it all" people. They think they have all the answers and should keep correcting people on everything, maintaining a sense of superiority. You shouldn't care about them because no one can know everything, and who are they to correct you in a situation only you understand.

A speedy snapshot - At a team meeting, one of my colleagues, who often acts like a self-acclaimed expert, interrupted me while I was explaining a project update. He kept insisting that I was wrong, even though he didn't have all the details and hadn't been involved in the discussions I was referring to, so you will get many like these and have to deal with it.

d. **The most popular today "Online critics"** – This is quite common now in the age of social media, where 62.6% of the world's population or 5.07 billion people are on social media and 259 million new users joining every year.

source (https://www.smartinsights.com/social-media-marketing/social-media-strategy/new-global-social-media-research)

These so-called online critics pass judgement based on your social media content without knowing any context, which is not fair.

I keep seeing in the news how people from the media or movie industry get affected by this group who are popularly called trolls, and many of them are suffering mentally or psychologically because of this trolling.

You should never care about them because online opinions are totally shallow, and they don't know your story.

e. **Wow, the most common ones: "The Gossipers"** – This is the most common group of people around us, in our family, in our neighbourhood, in offices everywhere. You can't get away from them. And this group of people loves discussing others' lives and spreading rumours to feel connected.

And I shouldn't tell you why you should avoid them at all costs.

f. **So-called "Perfectionists"** – So-called perfectionists are people who have impossibly high standards and criticise others who don't meet their standards.

Why you shouldn't bother here because perfection doesn't exist, we are made to progress not to gain perfection, and your journey is personal not a competition, so it doesn't matter.

g. **The status seekers** – They judge people based on their education, wealth or social status, and they look down on all those who look less successful, obviously in their own world, which is not real or right at least.

Why you shouldn't care about them because success means different things to different people, and you should follow your own path, not theirs.

And you will get them at almost all the parties talking about their expensive trips and designer brands, looking down on others who didn't seem to have the same lifestyle

h. **The comfort zone defenders** – They are fearful critics who are very uncomfortable with change, judging all those who take risks or do different things. Ah, I can't tolerate them.

And you should never care about them because their judgement is defined by fear and not insights. You do whatever you want, take risks, create something new, do large stuff, don't let their fear limit you.

Swift snap here - When my husband mentioned that he was thinking about leaving his high-paying job to start his own venture, the reactions from family and friends were quick and skeptical. Some relatives couldn't understand why he'd risk financial security for something uncertain, saying, *"Why leave a stable job? You're crazy to give up all that comfort for a new venture"*

i. **Helicopter Overseers** – Overprotective figures like parents, bosses, or authority figures who constantly evaluate your choices and think they know what's best for you, which is not the case all the time.

And if I must tell you that their judgement is always based on their own fears and as the in charge of your life, you should decide what is right or wrong.

Quick snap - when I chose to relocate for a job opportunity in a new industry, I remember my mentor who had always been protective, kept reminding me of the "risks" involved. He would say things like, *"Are you sure you want to make such a drastic change? This might not be the right move."*

j. **Self-Judger – the most dangerous one** - They are often critical of others because they struggle with their own self-worth and project their insecurities. And why you should avoid them, because their judgement reflects their own issues, not your value. Focus on your strengths instead.

It's real - During a recent project, a colleague who's often critical of others started pointing out flaws in my work, making me second-guess myself. At first, I took it personally, but then I realized that this person often struggles with their own self-esteem and tends to project their insecurities onto others. Instead of letting their judgement affect me, I reminded myself that it was about their issues, not my abilities.

Anyhow, these are the people who would judge you and create a sense of fear in you, but now you know that:

- Their judgement reflects their issues rather than yours. Most of the judgement comes from personal insecurities or biases rather than a real understanding of your life, so just ignore them.

- Judgements are very subjective based on someone's individual experiences and perspectives, but what matters is your own view.

- You define your worth, no one else.

You must be thinking, why sometimes our own family or friends judge us and don't support our growth? Let's talk about it then...

Now let's understand that our families have a certain place for us in their heart and life. When you grow, you are killing off the same person, and you are changing who you are. They are comfortable with who you are now, and when you decide to change or grow, they lose that space or place with you. So, they react or judge you in a negative way and don't support your growth. So, let's not judge people who are judging us, and everyone has a valid reason for it.

Why you shouldn't bother and waste your time on people judging you with no clue and who talk behind your back.

And remember that you don't need to worry about people who talk behind your back, they are behind you for a reason.

Chapter 8

Master 11 Blissful Practices to Overcome Fear of Judgement and Shine as Your True Self

Welcome to Chapter 8, a crucial moment in your journey towards authenticity and self-empowerment.

Till now, we delved into the nature of judgement, how and where it is rooted, and its pervasive influence on our lives. You met Mr Bliss – the cheerleader and your supportive voice that champions your true self. And Mr Blameworth – the critic that restrains your potential. Understanding these characters has been essential in reorganising how deeply judgement is ingrained in our daily experiences.

Now, we stand on the brink of the most crucial part of the book; it's time to take decisive action.

The techniques you are about to master are not just tools; they are your shield against the fear of judgement that holds you back from embracing the life you deserve.

These 11 powerful techniques will empower you to confront Mr Blameworth's negativity and amplify Mr Bliss's encouraging messages.

This section is vital because it transforms insights into action, allowing you to regain your voice, trust your instinct, change your mindset, take action to shield yourself from this judgemental world, and celebrate your unique identity.

By applying these strategies or techniques, you will learn to navigate the world with confidence and authenticity, breaking free from the judgement trap that has constrained you for too long.

So, are you ready to embark on this transformative journey? Now the time has come to take control of your narrative and live fully as your true self.

Let's dive in and equip you with the tools you need to make lasting change.

Your path to empowerment and authenticity begins now!

Let me first talk about the broader aspects or categories under which we are going to unlock these 11 techniques and why it is so.

Why Mindset, Action, and Reflection?

You might be wondering why I've categorised the techniques into three parts: Mindset, Action, and Reflection. Let me take you back to a pivotal chapter of my life to show you why this sequence is so important in breaking free from the judgement trap.

Sneak Peek Time – When I left my hometown, Jamshedpur, to join college in Vishakhapatnam, I was filled with excitement but also a lot of fear. Everything felt different – the language, the culture, even the way people carried themselves. My classmates spoke fluent English and participated confidently in discussions while I shrank into the background, convinced I wasn't good enough.

In those early days, I would find every possible excuse to avoid participating in class. If the professor asked a question, I'd look down, praying not to be called on. Group discussions were my worst nightmare – I'd skip them altogether, hiding in the library or pretending to be busy elsewhere. My fear of judgement held me captive, feeding into my belief that I didn't belong.

But then, something clicked. As I watched others participate and thrive, I asked myself: Am I really less capable, or am I holding myself back with my own insecurities? That question was the spark that shifted my mindset. I realised that if I wanted to grow, I had to start somewhere, even if it was uncomfortable.

The first step was daring to take action. I decided to raise my hand in class just once a day, even if my heart pounded. At first, I stumbled over my words and felt embarrassed. But I kept going. I joined a study group not to shine but simply to learn from others. Slowly, those small actions built my confidence.

At the end of each day, I reflected. I'd ask myself: What went well today? What made me uncomfortable, and why? What's one thing I can do better tomorrow? Reflection became my tool for self-improvement – it helped me see my progress and reminded me that my fears were often bigger in my mind than in reality.

By the end of my first year, something incredible happened, and I topped my class. It wasn't just about the grades; it was about the transformation I had undergone. The judgement I feared had lost its grip on me, and I was finally free to show up as my true self.

Looking back, I realise that this success came from following the exact process I'm sharing with you – starting with the right mindset, moving to consistent action, and finishing with thoughtful reflection. This sequence isn't just a method; it's a powerful way to break free from the judgement trap and unlock your full potential. Why does mindset come first?

Mindset comes first because:

- Mindset is the foundation of your belief system – your mindset shapes how you perceive yourself and the world. If you don't believe in your abilities, then taking actions can feel overwhelming. Therefore, having a positive mindset helps to build a strong foundation of self-acceptance and confidence, which is the key to authenticity.

- Replacing negative thoughts with other constructive ones – Beginning with focusing on mindset helps in identifying and overcoming self-limiting beliefs. To reframe means to change the view — more specifically, to get rid of the attitude of fear and look for ways to improvement.

- Emotional Toughness – A positive mindset is essential for emotional toughness. When you face criticism, feedback, or judgement, a strong mindset enables you to handle it well rather than going into a shell.

We will discuss this in detail in **"Mindset: Cultivating a Positive Inner World"**

Why Action Follows Mindset

Now the right mindset or understanding is only half the battle. Action is where the transformation truly occurs.

And here is how,

- By translating beliefs into behaviour – now you need to start translating the right beliefs into actionable steps. Taking action strengthens the new mindset, creating a cycle of growth. Every small action you take helps set your belief in yourself.

- Building Power – By actively engaging with the techniques, you can experience the benefits of your mindset shift firsthand, and this energy makes it easier to continue progress and reach the growth cycle for you to see the tangible impact.

- Facing fears Head-on – now taking action allows you to face the fear we are talking about in a very structured way. Instead of avoiding the situation or hiding from the situation that triggers judgement, you learn to face them. The gradual exposure helps you desensitise the fear and make it less daunting for you over time.

You will uncover all of this through the techniques.

Why Reflection is the Final Step

Reflection is the key to understanding your journey and learning from the experience.

By taking time to reflect, you will not only gain deeper insights into your goals but also recognise the patterns and celebrate your growth.

Why Reflection is Your Secret Growth Weapon:

1. Lock in the Learning

   - Reflection cements the lessons from your mindset shifts and actions.

   - It's like hitting "save" on your progress—celebrating wins and spotting areas to level up.

2. Discover Hidden Insights

   - Think of reflection as your personal progress tracker.

- It reveals how your thoughts, actions, and outcomes connect, giving you a clear path forward.

3. Fuel Lifelong Growth

- Regular reflection keeps your growth engine running.
- It helps you stay aligned with your goals and ensures you're always moving forward.

Why this Structure Matters

The goal in grouping the strategies into Mindset, Action, and Reflection is to provide you with a clear, step-by-step guide to escaping the judgement trap.

Crafting your personal growth blueprint: - Combine these strategies to unlock insights, build self-awareness, and make confident decisions.

The journey won't always be easy, but it will be worth it. Each step brings you closer to embracing your true self and reclaiming your life from the fear of judgement.

Together, let's set out on this transforming adventure!

Mindset: Cultivating Your Inner Compass

Our mindset is the compass that guides us in every step of our journey.

Shaping your life with intention helps you move through it with clarity and purpose, remaining untouched by the gusts of judgement or uncertainty.

By listening to your inner compass, you can always discover your true path, regardless of the opinions around you.

It's our mindset or wiring in our brain which defines the way we react to any judgement, criticism, or feedback.

Sneak Peek Time – I remember my journey in the early days of university and job when any criticism or feedback was a judgement for me. I used to take every criticism harshly and used to react in an adverse way to it.

If someone used to comment on my looks, dressing sense, intelligence, or skills, I used to feel miserable for many days, and that person is immediately out of my favourites or friends list.

Let's go back to my graduation days . Once I had to give a presentation on the topic of "DNA replication". I knew everything on the topic, and I loved the opportunity, but the issue was the language. I wasn't fluent in English and used to be afraid to talk to people there. This was the time I became an introvert from an extrovert.

Finally, the day came for the presentation. I gave my 100% with the content and presentation but couldn't express myself like many other classmates who were quite proficient in the language.

Many appreciated my effort, but the professor criticised me for my bad English, and his words were like a sword on me and shattered my self-image and confidence in front of my friends.

For many days after that, I kept feeling low and out of the zone; I used to bunk his classes and avoid meeting him in person. It took me a long to return to a normal state.

This happens to many of us, and I know many of you must be relating to it now.

Like many incidents, this happened after university when I went to Hyderabad for my MBA, and after that when I started looking for a job in 2009.

I remember how every criticism was like a trauma for me, and I used to hate myself before I hated the person who criticised me, and do you know why this used to happen?

Because of my mindset and how my brain was responding to each situation of criticism and feedback. At that point in time, every negative feedback or criticism felt like judgement, and every time, I used to talk to Mr Blameworth.

At that time, I never realised that Mr Blameworth was damaging my self-confidence and pushing me towards the wrong mindset.

If someone used to suggest or give me feedback that:

"Shalini, I think you should improve your English," then immediately Mr Blameworth used to whisper in my ear that, "This person doesn't like you and he is judging you; you should keep distance from this person." Mr Blameworth never missed a chance to damage my self-confidence and self-image after every feedback like this.

"Shalini, you must improve your presentation skills" – now you can guess what Mr Blameworth is going to put in my ear – he is not your well-wisher, he doesn't like you at all, and, given a chance, he would never promote you in your job.

So, it was I whose mindset was wrong and not the person who is giving the feedback.

It's a real struggle, and many are suffering from it now.

I wish I had communicated with Mr Bliss more in those days, anyway.

Now let me tell you why I used to react differently to feedback or criticism.

Why does our body respond when we encounter criticism with our nervous system?

How can a small criticism dent our self-image or perception?

Sometimes, criticism can give you a sharp pain, and sometimes you just feel okay and try to digest

You must have experienced a shooting pain when you hear a criticism with a feeling of anxiety and sensation in your stomach. Do you know that this happens due to the response of our autonomic nervous system?

Yes, it's our brain, nervous system, or mind that is inspired by our mindset to make this happen for us.

Let me explain this to you here.

So here, the autonomic nervous system has 2 branches: the Sympathetic nervous system (SNS) and the Parasympathetic nervous system (PNS).

Let's see the scenario – with **Sympathetic nervous system with Mr Blameworth.**

What happens when your SNS is activated with the "fight or flight or freeze" response.

When Mr Blameworth is active inside you and your best friend, then you react to everything, every comment, and situation, good, bad, or ugly.

So, imagine someone criticises you or gives negative feedback, immediately your Sympathetic nervous system gets activated and puts you in a "fight or flight or freeze" situation, releasing stress hormones like adrenaline and cortisol to prepare the body for immediate action. You may experience increased heart rate, rapid breathing, heightened alertness, and this takes you to a state of stress, anxiety, defensiveness, or aggression.

So, here is what happened.

What is activated – Sympathetic nervous system with fight or flight or freeze mode

What is the hormonal response – release of adrenaline or cortisol which prepares the body for immediate action

What is the emotional response – being defensive or aggressive, you might feel to give back or just leave from that place.

This is exactly what happened when we react to any criticism with a negative mindset or with your critic friend, Mr Blameworth.

Now the opposite scenario – **Parasympathetic nervous system with Mr Bliss**

Now, just imagine you are in a positive mindset, and you take criticism as a way to improve yourself. When you are close to Mr Bliss, your cheerleader, and see every comment to refine you, then in that case

When you receive criticism or negative feedback, this is what happens in your body.

When you hear criticism from someone,

What is activated – the Parasympathetic nervous system is activated with the "Rest and Digest" mode, which makes you relax and gives a feeling of recovering from a stressful situation.

What is the hormonal response – when the Parasympathetic nervous system kicks in, it helps to lower cortisol levels and heart rate, sending a calm signal to the mind.

What is the emotional response – if you engage with Parasympathetic nervous system after criticism and follow positive talks and mindfulness, you can handle criticism in a constructive way and only benefit from it.

If you understand this process as how your mindset can influence the way you react to a situation with your mind and body, you can easily make it work in your favour.

And this is the most favourite part for me in my own book.

And if you ask me a question, "What do you regret not knowing when you were younger?" my answer would be this page.

If I had known this secret of how my own mindset can make or break me, I would have avoided many stressful situations in my life.

Remember, Champions eat feedback for breakfast, and when they face criticism, their bodies don't panic – they power up. It's like their internal systems know that feedback isn't a threat; it's fuel for greatness.

Now, let's get into the techniques to get the right mindset to conquer the fear of judgement and move towards your authentic self 😊

Technique 1. BBM

Bestie Bliss Method - Make Mr Bliss Your Best Friend & Embrace Imperfection

Imagine for a moment you have a best friend, who is always by your side, whispering words of encouragement in your ears whenever you feel down or stressed with the fear of judgement.

He is the friend who is always with you irrespective of your trip or stumble, and he knows that growth comes with imperfections.

And that friend is **Mr Bliss.** The voice inside you that believes in your potential always reminds you that mistakes are good for growth and cheers for every little win.

Mr Bliss is the only person who will fight with Mr Blameworth, who is continuously feeding your fear of judgement.

The Bestie Bliss Method is all about choosing to listen to your supportive voice of Mr Bliss instead of letting Mr Blameworth take control.

It's about embracing your own imperfections as part of your unique story and silencing the voice of self-judgement.

Choosing Mr Bliss is choosing self-compassion over self-criticism.

The best way to avoid indulging in the game of fear or being judged is to make a strong bond with yourself or Mr Bliss, just like the connection you would have with your best friend.

If you make yourself your best friend or ally, then external judgement loses its power, and in this case, it's Mr Bliss

Make Mr Bliss your trusted companion and best friend, someone who always has your back and supports you unconditionally in any given situation. The more you talk in the form of positive affirmations with Mr Bliss, the stronger your bond will grow.

Remember, your relationship with your positive self or Mr Bliss is a matter of practice. The more you work on this, the better it works for you, and it's a lifelong relationship that never fades like any other relationship.

We all know that we can't stop external noise, judgements, or opinions, but we can deal with it with ease with Mr Bliss.

Let's see the benefits of making Mr Bliss your Bestie

- Solid positive support – Make sure you talk to Mr Bliss regularly when he reminds you of your strengths, doesn't allow you to get drowned in fear or negativity. Whenever self-doubt creeps in, he is there to remind you that "you have got this" or "your worth is not defined by others' opinion".

- Makes you less reactive to external judgements – Mr Bliss will help you deal with external reactions and instil the belief that others' opinions don't define your value.

- Will help you practise self-compassion – self-compassion is important if you want to avoid external noise and overcome the fear of judgement. Mr Bliss will help you focus internally and avoid the fear of being perfect in the eyes of others.

- Shifting focus on self-growth – Mr Bliss will keep pushing you to mind your own business and focus on your own growth.

- Truly embrace your true self – as your best friend, Mr Bliss, will encourage you to live authentically, making decisions based on your values rather than with a fear of how others judge you.

By making Mr Bliss your best friend, you can cultivate a mindset where your inner voice becomes your greatest cheerleader.

Now, you must be thinking how to do this all the time when you need it.

Here are the Steps

1. Invite Mr Bliss – Whenever self-doubt or judgement occurs, ask yourself this: What would Mr Bliss say? Try to silence that inner voice with Mr Bliss's resolve.

2. Change the Focus – When Mr Blameworth blames you for your past endeavours, concentrate on what you have gained from such experiences and the forward leaps you have made.

3. Appreciate Flaws – Encourage yourself that there is no perfect person, and therefore you do not have to be one because you are a perfect work in progress.

Quick Wins: Identify one fear of judgement you're dealing with and let Mr Bliss reframe it into an opportunity for improvement.

The next time you make a mistake (hopefully not today!), act quickly and think: What is the lesson here? Acknowledge that learning moment with joy.

Key Takeaway: With Mr Bliss as your best friend, you silence the judgemental self-talk, make room for and embrace imperfect growth, and transform fear into fuel for improvement and distance yourself from Mr Blameworth.

Watch Out For: Mr Blameworth creeps in with self-critical remarks. He will try to make you feel small, but remind him that your goal is "progress, not perfection."

What to Remember: Fear of judgement will melt away when you love and accept yourself with all your imperfections and mistakes, as a part of your journey. Mr Bliss will always be your cheerleader and ensure you do not stop moving forward... imperfections and all.

Technique 2. MMMM

2.Mind Mend Magic Method – Stop Negative Thoughts & Foster Quiet Confidence

Stop Negative Thoughts: When you think bad things about yourself, tell yourself something good instead, for instance - I am capable and deserving of success., Every step I take is progress toward my goals, I bring unique value to the table, I am proud of how far I've come, I am constantly learning and improving, my confidence grows stronger with each challenge I face, I am worthy of love and respect just as I am, I have the skills and determination to achieve great things, I am grateful for my strengths and embrace my individuality, I am enough, and I believe in my potential.

Now, when you have made Mr Bliss your best friend and he is your guide, then half of your fear is gone. But still, if you can't stop your negative thoughts or negative self-talk with fear of judgement, then **Mind Mend Magic method** will help you here.

One of the main reasons we start caring about others and get into the self-doubt and the extreme fear of judgement trap is due to negative self-talk, and the Mind Mend Method offers a practical and transformative way to deal with it.

Negative thoughts can be extremely detrimental and can damage your mind, followed by self-confidence and self-esteem, so start replacing your thoughts with affirmations that uplift and reinforce self-worth.

Negative thoughts are like unwelcome guests; they arrive without any invitation and will not leave until you throw them out. I know it's easier said than done, but the Mind Mend Method is the tool for doing just that.

It's about catching these negative thoughts as soon as they appear and replacing them with positive ones.

It's about replacing self-criticism with self-compassion.

The simple logic of this method is to replace your negative thoughts with empowering and positive affirmations.

Think of it like a mental switch: the moment you start thinking something negative, immediately switch it with positives and tell yourself something positive.

Over time, this practice mends your mindset, making you stronger and further away from the fear of judgement.

And the simple steps to do this are:

- First, identify the negative thoughts – what are these thoughts? Is it about your appearance, abilities, worth, or something else?

- Then challenge the negativity – ask yourself, is it based on some truth or facts? In most cases, it won't.

- Now counter with positivity – Now start replacing negative thoughts with the positive ones like "I am not good enough" replace with "I am capable and worthy of success and I know how to create it" or "I can achieve anything, nothing is impossible, and I know it". You need to replace self-doubt with self-encouragement

- Keep repeating it – and please be consistent in doing this to get the results.

Flashback Moment - Right after graduation, I stepped into my PGDM journey, battling self-doubt and a shaky command of English. Long presentations and extended discussions felt daunting, but I refused to let hesitation hold me back.

With consistent effort and the unwavering support of my incredible professors—Mr. Jitender Govindani, Mr. Zarar, Dr. Anil Ramesh, Mr. Qutub, and many others—I started finding my voice. They didn't just teach me; they believed in me, encouraged me, and challenged me to rise above my fears.

It was during this phase that I began to reclaim my confidence. A big part of who I am today is because of their guidance and the foundation they helped me rebuild.

Here you need to be specific, authentic, and consistent.

Our minds often trap us in self-doubt, laziness, and procrastination, convincing us we're unworthy. To break free, take control of your thoughts—if you can dream it, you can achieve it.

The **Mind Mend Method** builds self-confidence and self-esteem, fostering emotional well-being and motivation. Each time a negative thought arises, replace it with a positive statement. Over time, this practice nurtures quiet confidence—the self-assuredness that comes from within, free of external validation or show.

Quiet confidence is subtle yet powerful, helping you navigate challenges and handle difficult people with ease and authenticity.

Quick Wins:

- Identify one negative thought today and replace it with a positive one. Write it down and reflect on it; it changes your mood.

- Set a timer for 5 minutes and list 3 things you have done well today, no matter how small.

Key Takeaway: You have the power to mend your mind and transform it from self-criticism to self-compassion and self-kindness.

Watch Out For: Entering any uninvited negative thought as a guest, if this happens, immediately call your friend, Mr Bliss.

What to Remember: Negative thoughts are powerless if challenged. The Mind Mend Magic method helps you replace these thoughts with the positive ones and allows you to build a mindset focused on growth, not fear.

Positive thoughts stimulate the part of your brain that boosts resilience and optimism (Davidson et al., 2000), making it easier to let go of the fear of judgement.

Source **(Davidson, R. J., Jackson, D. C., & Kalin, N. H. (2000). "Emotion, plasticity, context, and regulation: Perspectives from affective neuroscience."** *Psychological Bulletin*, **126(6)**, 890-909.)

Technique 3. GGT

Growth Guardrails Technique – Set guardrails that keep you on the path of growth.

Now the "Growth Guardrails technique" is all about setting clear rules or boundaries which act like guardrails on a road, just like a guardrail that keeps a car from going off track.

Growth is never a straight line; it has a lot of twists and turns and many distractions on the way, and it's difficult to stay on the right track without a rail. Here is exactly the **"Growth Guardrails Technique"** to rescue you.

Here, the guardrail is the boundary you set to stay focused, protected, and moving forward, even if life tries to push you away.

I have tried this technique which worked magically for me. There was a time, probably in the initial days of my career, when I was just going with the flow, listening to all, full of self-doubt, always wanting validation from others if I was going in the right direction. I was unable to say no to people, and this was the time I was filled with fear of judgement and always used to walk with the thought "what will people say?" And then something changed inside me, and I created my Growth guardrail and followed it, and it was life-changing.

Are you curious about what these rules can be? Let me talk about some of my values and rules with one instance of how it worked for me.

- If authenticity is your value, avoid situations where you feel pressured to be someone else.
- Set a boundary that you will not stay in the office after 6 pm, unless it's critical
- Start saying no to people
- Limit social media to avoid distractions and others' judgement

These are a few rules, which were part of my "Growth Guardrail".

Now, let me tell you about one incident when I made myself stick to my true path and avoided being someone else.

Flashback time - In 2017, I joined a multinational organisation as a Marketing Manager with great responsibilities on my shoulders, and I was loving it. This was one of the highlights of my career when I shifted from Indian multinationals to an international multinational organisation. And this was possible with the help of one of my seniors or mentors with whom I had worked before. I was extremely happy and on cloud nine with my professional growth and stride.

I remember my first meeting with him as my manager post my joining. The first thing he asked me was to be his eyes and ears, with an expectation to gauge around. I should be the first person to tell him what is happening on the office floor, which made me realise my inability to do it.

I was never the type of person to pass along information to the boss just to score some brownie points. Instead, I stayed focused on my work, dedicated to making a real difference. And I couldn't be the person he wanted me to be, because that was not me.

Let me tell you, my manager and the mentor respected this value of mine. In fact, he highlighted this as one of my positive traits during the review. This is just one example of how staying true to yourself, even under external pressure, can pay off, keeping you intact on your true path.

The guardrail is like putting your personal values and goals together intact with a non-negotiable rule on a path without any distraction, and this Growth guardrail technique will protect you from any fear of judgement or comparison going ahead on this path.

The growth guardrail is a clear path that will keep your growth on track and stop you from derailing, keeping your focus intact.

Growth guardrail plan is about creating (Steps)

- A clear boundary – very specific and personal guidelines for yourself, and these can be about how you spend your time, how you achieve your goals and stop yourself from distractions. These guardrails ensure you are always moving in the right direction.

- With clear rules, stay focused on what really matters – when you have clear rules in place, the guardrail prevents you from meeting any accidents with distractions, doubts, and external pressures.

- Avoid options – Guardrails also simplify your life by simplifying your choices, because the more choices, the more you are distracted.

- Consistent efforts are important – this growth guardrail also asks you to be consistent on your path by sticking to your own rules without getting pulled in different directions.

- Protects you from external judgement – and finally when you set a clear boundary or you have a guardrail, you are less likely to be influenced by others' opinions because you have already decided what is best for you.

This guardrail also helps you decide what is okay and not okay for people to say or do to you, learn to say no and follow your own path.

The Growth Guardrail technique gives you structure, focus, and protection from distractions and pushes you to grow confidently without worrying about what others think or say about you.

Quick Wins:

- Write down your top 3 values and one boundary you will set today to stay true to them.

- At the end of the week, review one decision you made that kept you on your growth path.

Key Takeaways: Guardrails prevent distraction and keep you reminded of your values and goals. They protect your growth and help you stay focused on your true path.

Watch Out For: Compromising your values to please others.

Do not lose yourself to external pressure.

What to Remember: Your growth is your responsibility and journey, and you will have to own it by setting a growth guardrail that is aligned with your purpose.

Setting clear goals and boundaries strengthens your brain's focus and self-control, helping you stay on track for growth (Hofmann et al., 2012).

Source - Hofmann, W., Baumeister, R. F., Förster, J., & Vohs, K. D. (2012). "Everyday temptations: An experience sampling study of self-control.

Action: Taking Steps Towards Change

Now, after setting the right mindset or understanding, it is half the battle. Action is where the transformation truly occurs.

After identifying and understanding the mental barriers that are holding you back and fixing them with the techniques above, it's time to take action.

The Action section is all about turning insights into action and giving you tools and techniques to overcome the fear of judgement.

Taking action is where true transformation happens. Many people understand their fears but remain stuck because they don't take steps to confront them. This part of the book empowers you to make those moves, building on the inner work you have done and solidifying a new set of mindsets you have just realised here.

By applying the techniques, you start changing your behaviour after a change in the mindset.

Each technique in this section is designed to guide you in practical, manageable steps that lead to real change.

It's time to shift from understanding to doing, and with every small action, you are not only working to silence your inner critic but also actively rewriting or recoding your story.

4. Trusty Tap-In - Build Connections & Open the Reach-Out Path

First, let's talk about a few situations when and why you will need this technique.

Now imagine you are feeling stressed and overwhelmed with a big project at work and really need someone at your side, but you worry that asking for help might make you look incompetent?

Or imagine a situation where you have a presentation, and you are worried about how your performance will be judged by people.

Or are you struggling with a personal problem, a family challenge, or a health concern and feeling embarrassed to share these issues with others?

Or do you want to change your career or thinking to shift your work life but feel uncertain and worried about how others will perceive your decision?

In life, we all encounter moments when we need someone to lean on—a friend, mentor, trusted colleague, family member, or simply someone who truly understands us. Whether it's for emotional support or practical advice, having that anchor can make all the difference.

This is where the **Trust Tap-In Technique** becomes invaluable. It's about identifying and reaching out to those trusted individuals who can help us navigate challenges with strength and clarity.

I've been incredibly fortunate to have such people in my life— Mentors like Mr. Subroto Banerjee, Mr. Koustubh Kanade, Mr. Satish Dandekar, Mr. Narendra Deode, Mr. Rajakumar, Mr. Anil Sharma and many more, who guided me with their wisdom and experience. I am equally grateful for the unwavering support of trusted colleagues like Mr. Sridhar, Bhaskara, and Richa, who stood by me in professional challenges.

And then there are those who go beyond the professional sphere, offering a shoulder to lean on during personal struggles. For me,

Chaya Madam was one such person who extended her kindness and understanding when I needed it the most.

To all of them, and to everyone who has been a source of strength and guidance in my journey, I am deeply thankful. Their support has not only helped me overcome challenges but also inspired me to be a better version of myself.

Glimpse into Yesterday

This incident is from my time as a management trainee and sales representative at a leading Indian pharmaceutical company. As a gold medallist MBA graduate, I felt immense pressure to prove myself, don't know to whom, maybe to myself first and wanted to get into a management cadre in an organisation. However, I graduated during the 2009 recession, one of the worst in history, which forced me to compromise on the first role and job I had aspired to.

Recognising my performance, passion and drive to grow, my seniors and organisation offered me an opportunity to shift from my current sales profile to a marketing profile as a Product Manager; however, there was a catch. I had to pass an interview at the head office in Mumbai.

This was a critical opportunity in my life, and it left me feeling stressed and pressured to pass the test.

Now, at this time, I wanted someone who could understand me, empathise, and reassure me with "Don't worry, Shalini, just give your best and leave the rest," but no one did that.

I felt like I was in a pressure cooker and just wanted to escape.

I wanted guidance or just some soothing words from someone I trust and someone who really knew me and my situation.

This was the situation. I needed to tap in with someone I trust, reach out, and believe me on this, the fault was mine. I never made any connection with whom I can tap in, and I don't want you to be in such situations.

The trust tap-in technique is all about reaching out to someone you trust when you are falling or afraid.

Instead of keeping things to yourself because you are worried about being judged, this technique helps you overcome the fear of judgement and grow, and this starts with talking to someone you trust. Here is why it is critical:

- Emotional assistance – when you talk to someone you trust, you feel very safe sharing your feelings and you can easily deal with the fear of being judged.

- Less isolation – the biggest issue with the fear of judgement is that this makes you isolated and makes you feel alone because you don't share your thoughts with anyone. This technique encourages you to reach out, so you don't feel isolated. Just by realising that there is someone for you reduces the fear in life.

- Break this myth that asking for help is a weakness – if you have ever thought that asking for help is a sign of weakness, then you are wrong here; it's actually a sign of strength. The more you reach out to someone, the less you become scared of being judged. You should start feeling proud of being open.

- Fresh advice and perspective – when you talk to someone whom you trust, they can offer new perspective and ideas which can help you see things differently and make it easier to solve problems and move ahead.

- You have a regular tool for your growth – once you have learned to use this tool, you become very powerful. Regularly using this tool helps you realise that seeking help doesn't diminish your worth; this makes you strong, ready, open, and contributes to overall growth. The more you practice it, the less you fear being judged for your feelings and get more support on this journey.

This trust tap-in technique helps you break down the fear of judgement by being more open and emotional connection. This nurtures personal growth by encouraging you to ask for support from people who care about you and helping you move forward with greater strength.

The **Trusty Tap-In** technique encourages you to lean on trusted allies and build a support network. Having people to turn to, whether in a moment of doubt or triumph, strengthens your mental state and, most importantly, helps you overcome the fear of judgement.

And let me tell you about the simple steps by which you can always keep your friend ready with you.

- Identify trusted buddies – first make a list of people who qualify here.

- Reach out regularly – and always be with them or keep in touch regularly. Just don't expect them to be with you, but also be there for them when they need.

- Ask for help – whenever you are in self-doubt or happy or need someone to talk to, ask them.

Quick Wins: Send a message to someone you trust today and connect when needed.

Key Takeaway: You're not alone in your journey. Reaching out for support helps you gain perspective, boost your confidence, and stay focused on your growth, especially when fear of judgement arises.

Watch Out For: Don't hesitate to ask for help, thinking you'll burden others. Your trusted allies want to support you, and reaching out strengthens your bond with them.

What to Remember: Studies show that strong social connections significantly reduce stress and increase resilience (Cohen & Wills, 1985), making it easier to navigate challenges and fears of judgement.

5. Confident voice code - Speak Up with Confidence & Embrace Differences

At one pivotal moment in my life, I stepped out of my comfort zone, leaving Jamshedpur behind to pursue my studies in Vizag—a city miles away from everything familiar surrounded by people from different backgrounds and cultures. I had no confidence and no idea how to navigate this new environment. I listened to everyone around me without realising that I needed to stand up for myself.

People judged me based on my language and where I came from, and I didn't know how to defend myself. Back then, I didn't understand the value of differences or the importance of learning from others.

I know many of you have faced, or are facing, similar challenges in life when you are being targeted and you have no voice for yourself. You are holding back because you have no clue how to talk to yourself.

The **Confidence Voice Code** encourages you to find your own voice with assertiveness while respecting others' perspectives. By expressing yourself confidently, you set boundaries, communicate your needs, and stand up for what matters.

I remember days when I always used to say yes to all, never used to put my opinion on the table because I didn't know how to talk confidently . But now I realise this was the key to growth, and here is how it's done.

- Find your voice - Start by identifying situations where you tend to hold back. Practice speaking up in low-pressure environments to build your confidence.

- Set Boundaries: Assertively communicate your needs but be mindful of maintaining respect for others' views.

- Embrace Differences: Practice listening actively when others share their opinions, acknowledging their perspective even if you disagree.

Quick Wins: In your next conversation, try to share an opinion you usually keep to yourself. Pay attention to how it feels to assert your perspective.

Key Takeaway: Advocating for yourself doesn't mean being aggressive – it's about ensuring your voice is acknowledged and valued. Striking a balance between confidence and empathy only improves communication and deeper connections.

Watch Out For: Excessive explanations or unnecessary apologies for your beliefs. Communicate clearly, own your viewpoint, and have faith in its authenticity.

6. Technique DDD

Digital Detox Dial-Down: Mute the Digital Noise and Appreciate Real Moments

Today, information overload on the internet is causing more harm than good for many of us, specifically when we're seeking guidance or have unresolved questions. For instance, one day I wanted advice on how to dress with a particular colour combination. I found multiple views that were contradictory, which only added to my confusion.

In the present times, in the so-called Digital Age, young workers may be filled with a lot of information to keep abreast of trends in the industry, self-improvement, or even with the news.

The endless notifications from different people at their best holiday destinations or wedding destinations, or putting their best pictures of promotions, new cars, or their best dress, and many on the internet bring about frustration. Moreover, when people immerse themselves in scrolling through social media, they may tend to feel inferior to others due to their 'achievements', which lowers their self-worth.

My turning point tale - I distinctly remember a time in my life when the constant barrage of information and images on social media made me feel overwhelmed. Every day, I'd scroll through endless updates of people's vacations, promotions, new cars, and perfect moments, and it seemed like everyone was moving ahead while I was stuck in place. The more I saw, the worse I felt. I found myself questioning my own progress and achievements, and my self-worth began to take a hit.

It was a wake-up call for me. I realised that while information is vital in today's world, overconsumption of it, especially through social media, wasn't serving me. Instead of feeling motivated, I was feeling more distracted and disconnected from my true goals. I decided to take a step back and create some space for myself – intentionally disconnecting from the noise. I began dedicating time each day to silence the digital distractions, focusing on the things that truly mattered to me: my family, my personal growth, and my career aspirations.

This break gave me the clarity I needed to realign with my purpose and move forward with greater focus and confidence. I also realised the importance of curating the information I took in—only consuming content that added value to my life rather than comparing myself to others. It was this practice of purposeful engagement with the world around me that restored my peace of mind and helped me make more informed, empowered decisions.

In the end, it wasn't the constant flow of notifications or the pressure to keep up that defined my success. It was about choosing how to engage with the world and finding the quiet moments to reflect, reset, and recharge.

The **Digital Detox Dial-Down** technique encourages you to step back from screens and social media, allowing you to reconnect with the present moment and the people around you.

In a world filled with digital distractions, this practice helps you plant mindfulness and reduce the fear of judgement often amplified by online interactions.

Steps

1. **Schedule Breaks**: Set specific times during your day to unplug from devices—whether it's an hour in the morning, during meals, or before bed.

2. **Engage in Real-Life Activities**: Replace screen time with activities that bring you joy, such as reading, exercising, or spending quality time with friends and family.

3. **Reflect on Your Experiences**: After your digital detox periods, take a moment to reflect on how you felt during that time and what you noticed about your surroundings. In the beginning, you may find it challenging to disconnect from social media, as it has become such a constant part of our lives. However, with a bit of effort and consistency, gradually making this a habit can be truly life changing.

Quick Win: Try a "social media-free Sunday" where you don't check any social platforms. Notice the impact it has on your mood and interactions.

Key Takeaway: Reducing digital noise helps you reclaim your focus, enhances your relationships, and fosters a greater appreciation for real-life moments, helping to mitigate the fear of judgement that often arises from online comparisons.

Watch Out For: Don't fall back into the habit of mindless scrolling. Be intentional about your digital consumption and prioritise meaningful connections.

What to Remember: Research indicates that excessive screen time is linked to increased anxiety and depression (Twenge & Campbell, 2018). By moderating your digital interactions, you can enhance your well-being and cultivate a more present and fulfilling life.

Technique 7. TTT

Tiny Triumphs Tactic – Dream big and celebrate each milestone

Now, when you have taken care of your negative thoughts and also set boundaries for your growth, it's time to celebrate that and your win.

When you do something good, even if it's small, give yourself a pat on the back.

The fear of judgement can be paralysing with the fear of how others might perceive your work, idea, or actions.

The "Tiny Triumph Approach" is designed to help you reduce the fear of judgement by focusing on small and meaningful achievements rather than worrying about external validation.

Here, through this technique, I want to encourage you to celebrate yourself and small or tiny wins on a daily basis.

This sense of celebration will help you gain self-confidence, bring a sense of progress, and focus away from others' opinions.

Now imagine a scenario where you are preparing for an important presentation, and you are scared about it. Now, by using this technique, break the process into smaller pieces and enjoy smaller wins like

- For completing your first draft.
- For acknowledging your practice session.
- Reward yourself and party for showing up and speaking confidently, even if you are nervous.

By doing this, you become less concerned about others' opinions and more invested in your own progress.

And you must use it when you are enjoying new challenges like getting a new job or getting into a renowned university, in social situations or during your own personal growth like fitness or learning or doing a course.

I know many would relate to this situation, in the fitness journey first celebrate that you have started going to the gym for 3 days each week and then plan the next tiny milestone.

Sometimes, we take on bigger goals and lose ourselves in the visualisation process itself, so this is a tiny but very effective technique.

And here is how it works (practical steps for you):

- Instead of worrying about external judgement, look inside of you – yes, stop thinking about what others must be thinking. Your smaller achievements, no matter how insignificant they are,

are worth celebrating. Now, in the same situation when you are worried about how your colleagues might react to your new ideas, celebrate the courage you took to express and present them.

- Self-validate yourself – this fear arises when we seek validation externally. Imagine a scenario where you no longer seek external validation. By rewarding yourself for small victories, you will gain self-assurance, leaving no space for the fear of judgement.

- Develop flexibility in judgement – by consistently acknowledging your small wins, you start to build strength. The more you appreciate and celebrate your own progress, the less you are impacted by others around you.

The "Tini Triumph approach" is a practical and positive way to stay motivated and free from the fear of judgement. It's a good way to take control of your life.

Quick Wins: Start a "Tiny Triumph Journal" and add to it daily for a week, and you will be surprised to see how many small wins you have in your kitty.

Key takeaway: Start recognising your smaller wins and celebrate, because when you pat your back and celebrate yourself, you signal your mind that you are successful and shift your mindset from fear of failure.

Watch out for: Never ever think that your wins, however small, are just a coincidence or that you were just lucky. When you celebrate yourself, your brain receives positive reinforcement to build confidence.

What to remember: Research shows that celebrating small achievements boosts motivation and happiness (Frederickson, 2001), reinforcing your journey toward a more confident and authentic life.

Reflection: Deepening Self-Awareness

Now one of the most critical trios is Reflection, which offers everything if a person aspires for a change and self-improvement.

When Mindset assists you to develop the right conviction and Action motivates you to proceed in the direction of change, it is, however, the Reflection which allows you to comprehend, assimilate, and improve those efforts. This is the reason why it becomes an essential component in the "Mindset, Action, Reflection" triad – Action remains superficial and passing in its impact without it.

Why Reflection is Important

- Decrease the Need to Centre in Other People: In the instance of reflection, a person is offered resources to "think" about their feelings, thoughts, and behaviours at least at moments.

  It helps you identify that such things happen and that there is an effective way out of them, even if it feels like such patterns are unbreakable.

- Enhance Knowledge Retention: You may decide to change your behaviour or make things happen; however, in the absence of reflection, one can easily return to previous patterns of behaviour.

  Reflection in turn ensures that you do not forget both the achievements and failures, making every experience an educative moment.

- Assure Change: By gauging the effectiveness of what worked and what did not, you are in a position to shift where necessary.

  You can adjust your mind and its actions, providing a systematic cycle of growth that changes over time.

- Develop Emotion Regulation and Control Skills: Understanding and examining your emotional reaction to yours and others' opinions, especially fright and criticism, provides you with an understanding to deal with it.

Why it's Critical in the Fear of Judgement

The fear of judgement thrives when we react without understanding. Reflection helps you pinpoint where these fears come from, how they manifest in your actions, and how to overcome them. It takes you beyond automatic responses, enabling you to think critically and grow beyond those fears.

Without **Reflection**, you might change your actions temporarily, but deep, transformative change—especially regarding self-judgement and the judgements of others—won't fully take root. Reflecting on your progress allows you to appreciate how far you've come and adjust your strategies to continue your growth.

8. Technique - Power Up Playbook - Know Your Strengths and stay strong

Have you ever found yourself constantly comparing your life to others, wondering why you don't measure up?

Most of us constantly compare ourselves to others, thinking, "I wish I knew that" or "Wow, this person is so cool. I wish I were like them, as qualified or as brilliant." I, too, spent a large part of my life in that same mindset, unaware of my own qualities and strengths.

The irony is that many people overlook their own strengths, capabilities, and goodness, focusing instead on what others have. This constant comparison eats into their confidence, bends their perception of the world, and leaves them more vulnerable to judgement.

If you are also in the same mindset, then stop and think about it with these questions,

Why do I constantly compare myself to others, and how can I stop this habit to focus on my own strengths and build confidence?

How does comparison to others erode my self-worth, and what mindset shifts can help me trust in my abilities and stop seeking external validation?

How can I admire others without feeling inferior, and why is focusing on my own growth and happiness essential for personal fulfilment?

What practical steps can I take to recognise my own strengths and protect myself from feelings of lack or fear of judgement?

So, the first reflection you need is "to know your strength and nurture it."

Knowing your strength is crucial because this shields you from the fear of judgement and attaining your true potential for many reasons.

- Organically built unshakeable confidence - This type of confidence grows naturally from recognizing your strengths and areas of expertise. It's rooted in a deep belief in yourself, one that remains unaffected by external opinions or criticism. And remember, confidence should be your first line of defence against the fear of judgement because it helps you trust your abilities and decisions.

- Nurture genuineness – when you know your strength, you don't try to fit into others' opinions and expectations, and this authenticity is your next line of defence.

  When you are authentic, you don't try to seek validation in everything you do.

- Makes you mentally and emotionally strong – when you know yourself and your strengths, it's easy to bounce back from any adverse situation and the fear of judgement loses its grip on your mental and emotional well-being.

- Empowered decision-making – with a clear understanding of your strengths, you make more confident decisions and can take calculated risks and grow.

Knowing your strengths and staying strong creates a protective barrier against the fear of judgement, allowing you to focus on reaching your true potential without being held back by external criticism or self-doubt.

The **Power Up Playbook** helps you identify your core strengths and leverage them to stay resilient in the face of challenges, including the fear of judgement. When you recognize what you're truly good at, it builds an organically grown confidence—one that remains unshaken by external opinions or criticism. This inner strength empowers you to confidently navigate difficulties, focus on continuous growth, and handle criticism with grace.

Additionally, it equips you with the confidence to acknowledge when something is outside your expertise and seek help from others without hesitation, strengthening collaboration and fostering growth.

Steps

1. **Identify Your Strengths**: Take time to reflect on your key skills and qualities. You can use personal feedback, past achievements, or even personality assessments to identify your core strengths.

2. **Leverage Your Strengths**: Once you know your strengths, look for ways to use them in your everyday life. Align your actions and decisions with these strengths for greater confidence.

3. **Stay Strong**: When fear or doubt arises, remind yourself of your abilities. Trust that your strengths will carry you through challenges.

4. **Quick Win**: Write down 3 strengths you're proud of and keep them visible throughout your day. This will help you stay grounded in who you are.

Key Takeaway: Knowing and using your strengths is like having a personal toolkit for success. It boosts your self-confidence and helps you stay strong when facing external judgement.

Watch Out For: Avoid focusing too much on weaknesses. While it's good to improve, staying anchored in your strengths will keep you more confident and positive.

What to Remember: Research shows that focusing on strengths boosts well-being and productivity (Clifton & Harter, 2003). By recognising your unique qualities, you can reduce self-doubt and maintain resilience in the face of challenges.

Mantra: Find your core strengths and stay focused on them; keep refining and polishing.

9. Here and clear method - Stay Present & connect deeply

Try to think about what's happening right now, not what might happen later.

Here and clear method is an effective technique for reducing the fear of judgement by helping you focus on now and build confidence.

Now you must be thinking about when and how to make use of this. Remember that only practice can make you a master in this.

Imagine situations like:

- Having a big presentation or pitch in your job or for your business.

- When starting a project.

- In a challenging situation when you need to share an opinion and make decisions.

- Or in daily life when you are not feeling comfortable and there is a sense of fear around.

And here is how it will work for you:

- Grounding in the present – this method emphasises the importance of bringing your attention back to the present moment, and this involves noticing your surroundings and appreciating it.

- Mental clarity – By focusing on the present, you clear away distractions and allow yourself to focus on the present, which also stops your fear about the future and related issues, which is the basic problem here.

- Using techniques like Mindful breathing – Practising deep and conscious breathing brings you back to the present moment.

- By bringing body awareness – bringing yourself back from your future self and preparing yourself in the here and now.

- A focused mind – directing your focus on the task you are doing now and not thinking about the future.

I know this is easier said than done, but practice can make this work.

By using the method of "Here and Clear", you can reduce stress, increase your focus and improve overall well-being.

"Here and clear method" is very useful in reducing the fear of judgement by:

- Shifting your focus from the future or past to the present

- Better confidence by being clear in your thoughts and being self-assured about the situation

- Reduces overthinking – by being in the now, you tend to reduce the potential negative judgements and impact of these fears

- And finally, the most important thing that I want from all of you is to encourage you to live an authentic and confident life.

And this can be practised in simple **steps** like below:

1. **Take a Deep Breath**: Inhale deeply through your nose, hold for a moment, and exhale slowly through your mouth. Repeat these two to three times to centre yourself.

2. **Look Around**: Notice 3 things you see around you. Focus on their colours, shapes, and textures. This helps anchor you in the present moment.

3. **Engage with Others**: When talking to someone, listen actively. Nod or give small verbal acknowledgements to show you're engaged, which deepens your connection.

Quick Win: Set a timer for 5 minutes each day to practice mindfulness. Focus on your breath or a specific sound around you to ground yourself.

Key Takeaway: Staying present helps you let go of worries about what others think, allowing you to embrace your authentic self without fear.

Watch Out For: Avoid getting lost in distractions. Make a conscious effort to put away devices or other distractions when practising mindfulness.

What to Remember: Research shows that mindfulness can reduce anxiety and improve emotional regulation, and you can combat the fear of judgement and foster a deeper connection with yourself and others. (Clin Psychol Rev. 2011 Aug; 31(6): 1041–1056.)

10. Fall Forward Formula - From Challenges to Change

Have you ever faced a challenge that, with the benefit of retrospection, turned out to be a turning point in your life?

My turning point tale – Yes, I have. And it was a defining moment in my life, which had left me broken at the initial times. I really wanted to join a prestigious organisation in Bangalore. I thought this would be the next big leap concerning my work in the advancement of my career. I invested great effort into preparing for the interview, and really, everything in my presentation just poured from my heart. I had a future that I saw myself having success and impact, and I thought this job role was the key opening to all the doors to my dream.

Out of 8 rounds of interviews, I passed all 8. In the last discussion with the HR head regarding the appointment, I was rejected. To my surprise, I was informed that my vision was too large and idealistic for their present structure, and my aggression towards my career is not suitable for the role.

I would never have imagined how receiving that rejection almost crushed me; it felt like it was happening to me. Rejection makes you question your capabilities and even your dreams. Not for weeks but for months, I struggled with the disappointment, hitting a wall in my career. But with time, when I let myself reflect, new perspectives began to emerge.

I realised that the defeat marked the end of the journey, but for me, there was a fork in the road. If I had got that job, I would have ended up in Bangalore and never landed in the dream city Mumbai - City of Energy, Diversity, and Endless Possibilities. A place that changed my perspective for life and the world.

I never thought of what doors would open by shifting to Mumbai. The moment I reached Mumbai, I found the most vibrant community with a scope of working in a dynamic environment that helped in catapulting my aspirations further; work started providing direction in life and then began in ways I always planned and visualised them. If I ever look back, I really am grateful for that interview rejection. It broke me at that point in time, but it also set me free.

And from that day this is my favourite formula, and if it worked for me, then it can work for you as well.

Never be afraid of making mistakes; a person who makes mistakes is the person who is trying.

I remember one of the lessons from my mentor, Raja Sir: if you're not making mistakes and nobody is criticising you, then you're probably on the wrong path. So, if you are not making mistakes on the path of growth, then you are not growing in the right direction. Mistakes are our biggest friends; they tell us what not to do in life.

Learn from Mistakes: If someone tells you something you did wrong, try to learn from it and do better next time.

We are not made to do perfect things, we are made to make mistakes, learn, and progress.

Life is full of ups and downs, but it's essential to embrace setbacks as opportunities for growth. The Fall Forward Formula encourages you to view failures as stepping stones to success, allowing you to learn and adapt in the face of adversity.

Let's start doing it with the following easy steps:

1. **Acknowledge Your Setback:** Accept the reality of your situation without self-judgement.

2. **Reflect on the Experience:** Consider what you learned from the setback. What insights did you gain about yourself and your aspirations?

3. **Reframe Your Perspective:** Shift your focus from the failure itself to the opportunities that may arise from it.

4. **Take Action:** Use your newfound insights to create an action plan for moving forward, whether it's pursuing a new opportunity or developing your skills.

5. **Celebrate Small Wins:** Recognize and appreciate the progress you make, no matter how small.

Quick Wins

- Write down 3 lessons learned from a recent setback.
- Share your experience with someone you trust, turning the conversation into an opportunity for growth.

Key Takeaway: Every setback holds the potential for growth. Embrace your challenges, learn from them, and let them guide you towards your true path.

Watch Out For: Avoid dwelling on the negative aspects of the setback. Instead, focus on how it can shape your future.

What to remember: Let's enjoy being wrong, we can only learn new things and enjoy different viewpoints when we love and accept that we cannot be right all the time, and this growth mindset will keep fuelling us to move forward. Remember, being wrong is an opportunity to learn something new.

No one likes someone who is always right, being wrong is fun, being wrong is relatable, and being wrong and accepting it is the new cool"

Technique 11 Growth Over Gaze - Focus Internally, Not Externally

This is one of my favourite techniques, where we can really bring a lot of change in ourselves and the circumstances around us.

In a moment of reflection, I discovered that my path was uniquely mine, shaped by my experiences and aspirations. This realisation sparked a transformation; I began to prioritise my growth over external validation. By nurturing my inner world, I found clarity and strength to pursue what truly mattered to me, leading to fulfilling outcomes that aligned with my values.

This technique is encourages us to focus on learning and growing, instead of worrying about what others think and aims to enhance your focus on getting better at what you love and finding out how to feel better about yourself and worry less about what others think.

Now let me tell you a few steps to simplify the process, which would help you execute this in your life.

- First, focus on yourself – instead of caring about what others are thinking about you, put your energy into improving yourself. When you start growing well in life, external noise starts fading.

- Grow inner confidence – once you start growing internally and stop gazing at what others are thinking and saying, your confidence starts improving automatically, and this is what matters the most.

- Stop seeking approval from others – one of the reasons the fear of judgement comes from seeking approval from others. When we seek approval from others, we tend to be fearful of judgement, so stop doing this to get over this fear.

- Take judgements as feedback – whatever you do, people will judge you so try to take judgements as feedback which will help you improve, and this is about learning and not pleasing others. It's a thin line which we need to understand.

- Embrace Mistakes - Mistakes are valuable learning opportunities. Instead of avoiding them, embrace them, make mistakes, learn from them, and grow stronger with each one.

The growth-over-gaze technique asks you to focus on yourself and your own journey rather than others with simple steps like:

- Recognise External Triggers: Identify situations, social media accounts, or environments that prompt you to compare yourself to others.

- Shift Your Focus: Consciously redirect your attention to your own goals, values, and achievements.

- Practice Self-Reflection: Spend time journaling or meditating on your unique path and the progress you've made.

- Set Personal Benchmarks: Create your own measures of success based on your aspirations, not societal standards.

Quick Wins: Write down 3 things you appreciate about your journey that are uniquely yours.

Take a break from social media for a week to minimise external comparisons.

Key Takeaway: Your journey is your own. By focusing on your internal growth, you'll cultivate a stronger sense of self and purpose.

Watch Out For: Avoid falling into the trap of comparison. It can lead to feelings of inadequacy and distraction from your true goals.

What to Remember: The more internally focused you are, the less afraid you are of the external world.

Chapter 9

The Secret Mathematical Formula for Freedom from Judgement

I have never been a fan of maths but always of the formulas. Formulas are shortcuts and handy tricks, which you can easily remember at the time of application, and this always works at any age.

Here is the secret formula to get freedom from judgement:

$$(A^2 + S + P + A + B = FJ)$$

Awareness + Acceptance + Self-compassion + Perspective + Action + Boundaries = Freedom from Judgement

Now, let me explain each element of this formula to you.

A - Awareness – First, be aware and recognise when and where random judgements affect you. Notice what holds you back.

A - Acceptance – Accept yourself and know that no one is perfect in this world and we humans are not made to be perfect, we are made to progress. And accept that we all experience judgement at times in life and this will keep happening.

S – Self-Compassion – Be kind to yourself, and be your best friend and know that you are doing your best

P – Perspective – when you are conscious about someone's judgement, then ask yourself, "Does this really matter to me in this universe?" Focus on what matters to you now and not on what others think about you.

A – Action – Act towards the goal and act even when you feel judged. And remember that progress matters more than perfection.

B – Boundaries – Set healthy boundaries with people who are judgemental and hampering your wellbeing. It's good to ignore them or create distance from them. Please remember their judgement is because of their state of mind and not yours. Prioritise your mental and emotional wellbeing over what others are thinking about you.

And finally, the other part of the formula, if you apply all these elements well, is

FJ – Freedom from Judgement – If you follow all the elements from the first part of the formula, then you can live your authentic life. Putting this together, life will reward you with a confident and authentic life.

Do what you love and what gives you happiness, live your passion, set goals and pursue it. If you are busy doing these, then I don't think this fear can create any impact in your life. When we do not focus on our life and allow our mind to roam and think and feel any random thing, then only this fear can scare you. So keep your mind busy with better things in life.

Now, if you are like me and can't remember longer and lengthier formulas and need shorter ones, then this is another alternative formula to avoid the fear of judgement.

$$(S^3 = U)$$

Isn't it easier to remember

And here it is:

S – Spot – notice when something creeps in or disturbs you – catch it in the act.

S – Settle – show yourself some kindness - treat yourself like a friend.

S – Switch – Change your context and perspective – judgement is just a noise, not the truth.

And if you follow these 3 S, then the U is.

U – Unstoppable You – nothing can stop you from being great.

I am confident that you are going to use these formulas to break this trap with ***#judgementfreecode***.

Chapter 10

Why Embracing Boldness Early Leads to an Authentic Life - Priceless Lessons from My Youth

If you have come this far, then you are on the path of transformation and serious about your growth. Your future is bright if you can implement a few of these tips from your early age. By doing this, you can save time and avoid unnecessary struggles. While I believe that life teaches us everything through experience, we often learn these lessons too late—by then, half our life has passed. So why not start learning now, enjoy life, and avoid constantly trying to prepare for the future. And here we go.

1. Start celebrating yourself early in your life without showing it off to others, and no one should remind you of this.

2. Start rewarding yourself early in your life for every small win or achievement

3. Prepare yourself to receive while giving to others - Giving is important in life, but also make sure you receive love and respect

in return. If you are just giving with no gain, then create a safe distance.

4. Prepare yourself to take care of yourself - Create a kindness toolkit for yourself first, don't be harsh on yourself and practice self-compassion.

5. Consider mistakes as your stepping stones - Whenever you make mistakes, you will feel disgusted but see this as another experience in your kitty as what not to do in life.

6. Know a lot of people without stressing yourself to network – If you are a kind person, then this will happen without any effort.

7. Use curiosity as your compass - Keep exploring new knowledge and experiences through books, hobbies, and conversations—these will lead to valuable discoveries and personal growth.

8. Use your intuition and goals as your GPS system - Trust your gut feeling to help you navigate and, at the same time, have goals to guide you on the road of life.

9. Feel confident until you are - Feel confident because you are, and this doesn't come from external validation; this comes from knowing and discovering yourself.

10. Dare without doubts – Have fewer doubts and use your fear as fuel.

11. Remember that vulnerability is a strength – Don't be afraid to show your vulnerability; this shows your strength and not a weakness.

12. Look out for a bigger purpose in life – You can do much bigger things in life by distracting yourself from being judged or judging others.

And a bonus tip, which I have learned the hard way.

- How to identify a good person – whenever you meet someone and you feel big or valued, be with them or stay in touch with them, He/she is a good person.

- But when you meet someone and you feel small or inferior, make a distance from them. This person will only make you fragile and dent your confidence and eventually create a fear of judgement.

Remember, people can only give you what they have. A great person can give you greatness and make you feel big, and a damaged person can only give you emotional wounds. So, choose your crew wisely.

Chapter 11

How Ādhyātmikta (Spirituality) Can Create That Shield for You - Introducing "Spirituality Recode with Mr Bliss"

This is the closest part of me, and I love talking about how Adhyatmika or spirituality can create the shield you are looking for and can help you live a true and authentic life.

First, let me talk about Adhyatmika for a clear understanding and what it means.

The word adhyatma comes from the prefix adhi, which means "above or over", and the word atman, which means "spirit or soul".

Ādhyātmikta is the Hindi/Sanskrit word for **spirituality**. It refers to the search of understanding one's inner self (the *ātman*) and its relationship with the universe or a higher power.

Ādhyātmikta involves exploring deeper meanings of life, personal growth, and self-awareness, beyond material and worldly pursuits.

Let me share a glimpse of this colour from my own spiritual journey.

I understood this a couple of years back when I visited Kashi or Varanasi or Banaras with one of my close friends Deepti, and we called it our annual solo trip – a trip when we go to a place to sit quietly, reflect on our life, and feel our life very closely without any rush or responsibility of family or kids. . When I sat quietly, allowing myself to feel the universe and the powerful divine energy surrounding me, I connected to something greater than myself. In those moments of stillness, I could sense the vastness of the world and the endless possibilities it holds

I always lived searching for my purpose. I always used to think, "What am I contributing to this world?", "How am I making this world a little better or more authentic place?", "Is this all I can contribute to this world, or am I born to create something bigger for this world?" and used to ask the divine power, "Help me search for my bigger purpose in life."

When I visited Kashi, I went with the same question and wanted a hint from my divine power (Mahadev or Shiva), and I got my answer with thoughts when I was returning from Kashi, on the flight, when I was near him, technically.

There was a series of thoughts and concepts starting to come to my mind and I felt like a force inside me that wants to make it real, and this book is the result of that.

So, **Ādhyātmikta** or spirituality is not only about understanding oneself but also about receiving insights and guidance from a higher source to fulfil a meaningful purpose.

I was called to Kashi by my higher power to give me direction, and I feel his energy around me guiding on every tiny thing.

Ādhyātmikta involves exploring deeper meanings of life, personal growth, and self-awareness, beyond material and worldly pursuits, and far removed from any kind of fear.

When you are with your higher self, you don't fear.

When you are with your higher energy, you don't care about any judgement that can stop you from doing something significant.

In this book, I have shared my personal journey with you. I was once a person who felt untalented, vulnerable, and full of fear. The only positive trait I held onto was a deep desire to push beyond my limits and become more than I believed I could be.

And I feel spirituality, or **Ādhyātmikta**, helped me walk on this path and guided me towards self-discovery, helping me embrace my true potential.

Let's understand the fear of judgement from a spiritual perspective.

What is the fear of judgement – this fear of judgement is the deep-rooted need for external validation and acceptance. When we grow up, we are shaped by expectations and opinions of others, which creates a fear of rejection when we don't meet those standards. But Spirituality or Ādhyātmikta helps us understand ourselves first. And through self-awareness, we can break free from the chain of judgement.

Spirituality helps you feel more peaceful and balanced, guiding you to live in a way that feels true to yourself. It's about looking inward, finding inner calm, and focusing on what matters most to you—whether that's kindness, love, or a sense of belonging to the world around you.

When you are spiritual, the first thing that will change is you, the way you look at life and your outlook on life will change; everything and everyone will change later.

Spirituality or Ādhyātmikta plays a significant role in freeing you from any kind of fear. Would you like to know how?

- Connection to your inner self – the first change you will see is the self-reflection and inwardness, which will help you connect deeply with your authentic self. When you are very busy only looking outside or on social media, you can't see yourself.

- Disconnection from Ego – the next thing that will happen is you will start detaching yourself from ego, which is the source of fear of judgement. Because it's our ego that needs validation and fears rejection or failure.

- Compassion and Non-judgemental – Spirituality will make you compassionate towards yourself and others, and you will stop judging people without knowing their story. You will understand that everyone has their own journey and story.

- Focus on higher purposes – once you start being spiritual, you begin to focus on bigger goals or higher purposes beyond these superficial concerns of what people will say.

- Living in the present – spirituality teaches us how to live for today, and we mostly fear when we are in the past or the future.

- Confidence and inner peace – Once you are connected to your higher self, it strengthens confidence, you are at peace and you are more likely to act in alignment with your true self, regardless of external judgements.

How to get into the path of Spirituality or Ādhyātmikta:

There are ways you can practice embracing this path, which are easier to follow and work. It worked for me, and I am sure will also work for you.

1. Meditation – this is the proven way to connect with your inner self and higher self and detach from external noises or influences (I have started practising it, not much but just 5 mins. in a day).

2. Journaling – this is another way to practise, where you can write about moments when you've felt judged and explore why those judgements affected you. Use journaling to process your feelings and find spiritual insight (I practise this, I write down my thoughts and everything that comes across in my digital diary, and this book is also a compilation of that)

3. Gratitude: Practice daily gratitude for who you are, exactly as you are, without needing validation from others (I practice it daily within and I also have a gratitude jar where I put everything that created a spark in my life).

And studies have also proven that regular mindfulness practices, such as meditation, significantly reduce anxiety and increase self-acceptance. By integrating spiritual habits into your daily routine, you can improve the inner peace necessary to overcome the fear of judgement.

Research-Backed Impact of Spirituality

Mental Health: A journal named "Journal of Clinical Psychology" published a report in which it was stated that if you are experiencing anxiety and depression symptoms and engaging in spiritual practices like meditation and prayer regularly, it reduces anxiety by 30% to 40%.

Improved Focus and Creativity: Studies show that mindfulness meditation increases grey matter density in the brain, specifically in areas related to focus, emotional regulation, and creativity.

Increased Strength: Research by the American Psychological Association indicates that those who spiritual practice have better emotional toughness, which helps them in managing stress and recovering from setbacks.

How Spirituality Transformed the Lives of Influential Leaders

Spirituality has helped many influential figures develop personally, remain resilient, and succeed.

Take Oprah Winfrey, for example, who always claims that she never would have become the woman she is without meditation and her Attitude of Gratitude!

Steve Jobs based his managerial style in leading Apple on what he learned from Zen Buddhism, even teaching that it was his mindfulness that allowed him to create with such originality and vision.

After burnout, Arianna Huffington emerged as a spiritual guru, advocating meditation and mindfulness over mere achievement.

To improve his decision-making and manage stress, Ray Dalio, the Bridgewater Associates founder, used Transcendental Meditation.

LeBron James, for instance, uses meditation as part of his routine to improve his focus and be in the zone when he needs to hit big shots. The examples mentioned are testimonies to the fact that religious practices promote inner development and facilitate growth, balance, as well as success.

Spirituality Recode with Mr Bliss

Now when you know how spirituality can benefit, and given that it's a proven fact embraced by many throughout the ages, you might be wondering: 'I know it works, but how can I easily adapt it to my life and see tangible differences?'

If that's the case, let me introduce you to a practice that can truly change your life in a short amount of time, allowing you to feel the difference.

Introducing Spirituality Recode with Mr Bliss

Consider your brain as a very advanced computer that continually executes programmes on how you should think, act, and feel. A lot of these programmes provide good assistance, but a number of them, especially the ones related to the fear of being judged, may restrain you. These are like old programmes that no longer serve their purpose and keep telling you, "I am not worthy," or "What will others say?"—and prevent you from being yourself (remember our friend Mr Blameworth here, these are his words).

It is where "Spiritual Recode with Mr Bliss" comes into the picture.

It is more than just another idea thrown into the bunch; it is a fresh, exciting and fun solution in getting rid of those ingrained concepts and more so the fear of judgement.

We, therefore, understand that the actual strength does not come from the perspectives or ratings of other people but from the individual inner self. We stop being restricted by others and learn to be guided by our inner self without having to fit into structured society.

But here's the twist: you're not doing this alone. Here comes Mr Bliss who plays a critical part in the journey and is the one providing motivation. He is that voice of hope within you, infused with happiness, optimism, and inspiration. He has always been there to assure you that you are whole and capable of changing the limiting fear-based instructions in your head. He makes the work lighter and more enjoyable, transforming the daunting task of the process of spiritual recoding into a pleasant and constructive one.

Such that together with Mr Bliss, you begin a spiritual recoding transformation—doing away with those negative, judgemental thoughts and replacing them with positive, self-affirming thoughts. You will notice that people's views will start to concern you less, and more focus will be on your higher self, peace within.

You will be living with full self-acceptance, free from judgemental glares, and operating at the centre of your true self.

How to Practice Spiritual Recode with Mr Bliss – time to act now

We will do it in 2 major steps, and Mr Bliss will be in action here.

Action Steps for Spiritual Recode with Mr Bliss

1. Identify Limiting Beliefs

Practice: Take a moment to reflect on specific beliefs that fuel your fear of judgement.

E.g., "I'm not good enough" or "People will think I'm foolish." Write them down.

Ask Mr Bliss: Imagine Mr Bliss as your inner cheerleader, encouraging you to challenge these beliefs. Ask him what he would say to help you reframe these thoughts positively.

2. Recode Your Inner Command

Practice: Using the limiting beliefs identified, rewrite them into empowering affirmations.

Life lens

Change "I'm not good enough" to "I am worthy of love and acceptance as I am."

Ask Mr Bliss: Picture Mr Bliss cheering you on as you list these affirmations daily. His joyful energy serves as a reminder that you are capable of embracing your true self without fear.

Now, let me give you some more limiting beliefs and recode it with Mr Bliss

Limiting Belief: I am not smart enough to achieve my goals.

Recode : I am capable of learning anything I set my mind to, and my intelligence grows every day.

Limiting Belief: I will never be as successful as others.

Recode : I define my own success, and I am on a unique path that is perfect for me.

Limiting Belief: I am not worthy of love and respect.

Recode : I am deserving of love and respect just as I am, and I attract positive relationships into my life.

Limiting Belief: I always mess things up.

Recode : I learn from my experiences and grow stronger and wiser with each challenge I face.

Limiting Belief: I am too old or young to start something new.

Recode : There is no age limit on pursuing my passions; new beginnings themselves are an achievement.

Limiting Belief: I don't have the skills to succeed.

Recode : I am continuously developing my skills, and I have everything I need to succeed within me.

Limiting Belief: People will judge me if I fail.

Recode : I embrace failure as a stepping stone to success, and I trust my journey without worrying about others' opinions.

Limiting Belief: I can't change who I am.

Recode : I have the power to evolve and become the person I aspire to be.

Limiting Belief: I am not creative enough.

Recode one: I appreciate beauty around me, and that makes me uniquely creative

Limiting Belief: I am a burden to others.

Recode : I contribute positively to the lives of those around me, and my presence is a gift.

Limiting Belief: I don't belong anywhere.

Recode : I am worthy and deserve only authentic people around me

Limiting Belief: I'm not good at handling stress.

Recode : I am strong enough to manage it, and my friend Mr Bliss is going to help me here.

Limiting Belief: I am always anxious and can't overcome it.

Recode : I have the strength to manage my anxiety with calmness and confidence.

Limiting Belief: I'm not attractive enough.

Recode : I am different and beautiful, and I radiate confidence that attracts positive energy.

Limiting Belief: I must please everyone to be happy.

Recode : I prioritise my happiness and well-being, knowing that I cannot please everyone.

Why Combine Spiritual Recode with Mr Bliss?

The path to spiritual freedom doesn't have to be serious, lonely, or boring. With Mr Bliss, the journey becomes a joyful adventure.

Whether you're rewriting negative self-talk, practising daily affirmations, or meditating to calm your mind, Mr Bliss will be there, cheering you on every step of the way.

Think of him as your playful inner guide who believes in you completely—more than anyone else ever could.

Together, Spiritual Recode with Mr Bliss can be the key to unlocking a life where you no longer fear judgement, but instead, embrace the beauty of who you truly are.

Chapter 12

What are You Gaining by Breaking Free from This Trap?

This is important because by now you know what the fear of judgement is and how it can impact every aspect of your life. You have also learned how to get out of this trap and be your true authentic self in life because authenticity is a superpower, and you can only feel it when you have acquired it.

Now you must be thinking, what am I going to gain by breaking free from this fear of the trap?

If you have come this far, then you deserve to know this, but before we get into this zone, let me tell you a story.

There were 2 brothers near my place, the elder one was Mukesh and the younger one was Naresh. We were in the same age group and were staying in a single building during the early days of our life in Jamshedpur when everyone in that building was struggling to establish themselves in a fast-moving life (during the 90s even cities or towns like Jamshedpur or Tata Nagar were fast-moving cities).

Flashback Time"

I remember we used to spend a lot of time together after school and play in the Angan (the central open area of a house) and chat on the terrace. Mukesh was the elder one and one of the most intelligent people I had come across; he was excellent academically and in sports, a very responsible, kind, and helpful person. But I remember Aunty (his mom) always telling him to be the best and work harder in everything he does because he is the elder one and his younger siblings will only do well following him, so he has no other option but to succeed in life. I remember that whenever we used to meet in a crowd, everyone used to ask only Mukesh about his marks and how he is doing in his studies.

However, the younger one, Naresh, was a happy-go-lucky person, never bothered about anyone and quite good in sports. He was the child with the most absences in the school, and I had never seen him working hard either for his own studies or at home for anything else.

He was the younger one in the family with the least expectations and was most loved by almost everyone around.

And this always bothered me: why all the expectations from Mukesh and why nobody bothers Naresh with even a tiny hope.

I remember during festivals like Diwali, it was Mukesh who used to do all the preparations, and it was Naresh who was only busy playing and enjoying.

Now the twist and turn, Mukesh, who was the real talented one, always used to feel less confident. I had seen him bothered, thinking, "If I don't do well, then what will happen? How are people going to react?" and a deadly fear of being judged.

On the other hand, Naresh was less talented, not very responsible, with average skills and super high confidence. He was the witty one at home.

I had never seen him concerned about what others thought of me. He had no fear of judgement and wasn't very good in studies either. Quite the opposite character, I must say.Now, when you are visualising this story and the characters Mukesh and Naresh, you must be thinking: what are they doing now? What happened to Mukesh? Is he doing well in life? He must do well in life. And how about Naresh? Could he do something in life or not?

I feel you, so here is the twist.

Recently, when I visited my hometown, I asked my mom about them and how they are doing in life.

Now Mukesh, the talented one, is working in a government bank as a bank manager, married with 2 kids, and living a normal life in Jamshedpur.

And Naresh, the less talented one, is a business person owning a 100-crore organisation in Delhi.

Now, I know what you are thinking, and you always thought the most talented person is the most successful person in life, but this is unfortunately not true.

Mukesh being the most talented person, always lived under the pressure of others' expectations and with a deep-rooted fear of being judged, which always restricted him from self-expression, taking risks, and trying anything beyond boundaries. He always made decisions based on others' expectations or societal norms, and here he is safely landed in a government job. Society would never want you to do better than this. Mukesh was very creative but never tried anything unconventional in life, and most of the time, he looked to others for approval with a fixed mindset. Do you think he is successful in life and doing justice to his personality? Give it a thought

On the other hand, Naresh is a known businessman, and the way he is growing his business, very soon he will be an industrialist. Naresh is happily married with 3 kids, living a wealthy life in south Delhi with super expensive cars and a swanky lifestyle.

Naresh was always a happy-go-lucky person and never bothered about what others were thinking. He was expressive, daring, and always listened to his heart. He never used to censor his words and was honest with people. . He was willing to take risks and follow his heart, regardless of external opinions and potential failures.

Naresh did not bother much about others, which made him do bigger things in life without overanalysing it and without thinking about how others are judging him or will think about him.

I wanted to tell this story quite loudly to everyone, and there is no better place than this.

If you think talent and smartness alone can make you successful, think again. True success happens when your talent meets a fearless mind—a mind that dares to try, fall, and rise again without the weight of judgement. Talent gives you potential, but it's courage, resilience, and the freedom from fear that unlocks it. Only when you stop worrying about what others think and embrace the possibility of failure do you truly give your talent the chance to shine.

A fearful person behaves differently from a person without any fear of judgement. See the list below for your reference.

Sl. No.	Aspects of a fearful person and a person without the fear of judgement		
1	**Self-Expression**	Holds back, censors' thoughts	Freely expresses ideas and emotions
2	**Decision-Making**	Follows others' expectation	Makes authentic, value-driven choices
3	**Creativity & Innovation**	Plays it safe, avoids risks	Embraces bold ideas, innovation
4	**Relationships**	Seeks approval, struggles with vulnerability	Builds open, authentic relationships
5	**Social Anxiety**	Experiences anxiety in social settings	Feels comfortable and confident socially
6	**Response to Criticism**	Takes it personally, defensive	Sees criticism as feedback, learns from it
7	**Risk-Taking**	Avoids risks, stays in the comfort zone	Takes calculated risks, embraces challenges
8	**Mindset**	Fixed mindset values external validation	Growth mindset, focused on self-improvement
9	**Body Language**	Closed-off, anxious body language	Open, confident posture and movements

10	**Emotional Resilience**	Struggles to bounce back from setbacks	Resilient, less affected by negativity
11	**Life Choices**	Lives based on fear and external approval	Lives purposefully, aligned with passions

The key difference lies in freedom: a fearful person feels constrained by external expectations, while a person without fear of judgement experiences liberation, allowing them to live authentically and boldly.

There are many of you who only believe in proofs, data, and statistics; then, in that case, here are some benefits of breaking free from the judgement trap.

High Self-Esteem: According to the *Journal of Happiness Studies,* self-compassion is associated with high self-esteem among individuals. An estimated *70% of respondents reported a positive change in their self-concept after giving up self-criticism.*

Increased Creativity: *A study conducted at the University of California showed that those who manage to eliminate fears of judgement are 50 percent more likely to be creative, improving innovation and problem-solving ability in those people.*

Less Anxiety: Researchers in the Journal of Anxiety Disorders demonstrated a *40% reduction in symptoms of social anxiety among those actively working for 6 months on reducing fear of judgement.*

Better Decision Making: According to the study that was published in the *Harvard Business Review,* employees who are less judgemental are 30% more likely to opt for the decisions that would matter most to them and sustain the long-term goals.

Opportunities and Risk-Taking: According to *Gallup Studies,* people over being vulnerable with judgements of society make calculated risks-which may lead one to be promoted to the next rung up and moves into new areas of challenge and development.

Inspiration and Influence: According to Deloitte's survey, 65% of the respondents view individuals with authenticity and no self-judgement as inspirations who will chase after their own dreams.

Those studies reveal that when you break the judgement traps, you move towards your authentic self.

Chapter 13

The Upside of Judgement - Why It's NOT Always a Bad Thing

I know that Judgement is often viewed as a negative force because it limits our self-expression and alters how we see ourselves and others around. The overall effect is always limiting and disempowering. But (with a capital B) despite its many downsides, judgement can also serve as a medium to grow when approached with the right mindset.

When judgement is used wisely or constructively, it helps us grow and make the right decisions.

Threads of truth from my journey - I remember my journey in the initial 5 to 6 years of the job when I was in Hyderabad and Bangalore. Whenever someone used to criticise me or give some real feedback with improvements, including my seniors, it used to hurt me. I never took it in the right spirit and always used to feel miserable. If someone used to criticise me, that person was immediately on my non-favourite list. I used to avoid my critics because any feedback or criticism used to hurt me with a prolonged impact on my thought process and self-perception. Those were really tough days when there was no one to hold my hand

and explain why that feedback was my stepping stones, how I could have taken the criticism as tricks to improve myself.

And if you want to understand why we react the way we do to criticism, then please relook at chapter 8, where there are explanations of the reaction of our nervous system and how criticism affects our emotions and mental state.

Judgement is not always a bad thing because it serves important functions that can benefit us personally, professionally, and socially.

The right judgement can:

- Help us learn and improve – the right evaluation or self-judgement can help us spot mistakes and learn, e.g. – we can see the past actions and correct them in the future for our personal growth; this is also a judgement.

- Guides morally – Judgement helps us determine right or wrong, the kind of decisions we make daily in life. Our judgements guide us in doing things based on our set values, ethics, and principles.

- Encourages accountability – By judging actions, either our own or others', it helps us be accountable, and this is the basis of trust in relationships and also in society.

- Improves decision-making - Good or the right judgement is crucial for making decisions or informed choices. Here judgement is the right evaluation, and I don't think we can make any decision without using the right judgement.

- Offers constructive feedback - external judgements like feedback, if taken positively and delivered constructively, can provide great insights. E.g. - Feedback from a mentor, manager, or peers can point out blind spots, helping you grow in your career and personal life. This has helped me personally and professionally (thanks for your session, Daniel☐) both.

- Promotes critical thinking – Judgement allows us to assess the situations, ideas, or behaviour wisely, navigating complex situations.

- Motivates achievements – Constructive judgement can push us to strive for better results and growth, and this has helped me a lot in my growth.

  Here, if someone else also likes someone we respect evaluates our work or performance, it can motivate us to improve and reach a new standard.

- Inspires innovation – Judgement allows us to evaluate ideas and processes and guides us to improvements, new solutions, and breakthroughs because we can identify flaws and refine them.

- Now the most important and my favourite one – Judgement with the right mindset prepares you for the real world. And you know how, by learning how to handle and process the judgement, it helps us become more resilient. If we can develop a healthy relationship with judgement, then this helps us adapt and grow from those experiences.

Judgement when used wisely helps us in self-improvement, guiding values, accountability, better decision-making, constructive feedback, and can help us grow, protect our well-being, and function better in this society.

Judgement becomes a tool for growth, moral clarity, and better decision-making when applied wisely and it benefits us instead of holding back.

Chapter 14

How to transform judgement into your growth tool

As I mentioned in the previous chapter, judgement can be positive or negative, and it totally depends on how you take it. It's the mindset and attitude that make a difference, not the judgement.

If feedback you will take as criticism and talk to your Mr Blameworth, then he will give you multiple reasons to feel bad about it. However, if with the same criticism you talk to your cheerleader, Mr Bliss, then this becomes a reason to improve.

So, now you know how it works.

Now let's see how you can use judgement as a tool for your personal growth:

- Shift your perspective – instead of seeing judgement as a negative force, see it as an opportunity to improve. I know it's easier said than done but start doing it, you will feel the difference. When you receive criticism, ask yourself "what can I improve" rather than "why am I being judged". We will talk more about this in the next chapter with Mr Bliss and Mr Blameworth.

- Differentiate constructive vs destructive judgement – learn to distinguish between helpful and harmful; accept constructive judgements like feedback from a guru or mentor, grow, and ignore destructive feedback which can be harmful for you mentally.

- Be kind to yourself when dealing with judgement – Have awareness of your imperfections when dealing with judgement, instead of blaming yourself for mistakes, focus on how you can grow from them.

- Seek feedback from people you trust – ask for feedback from people you trust like your mother, father, siblings, mentor, peers, friends and be open to their insights and use the information in improving yourself.

- Turn judgement into an action – Don't let anyone's judgement disturb or paralyse you, use this as a motivator and not in defining your worth. If someone points out a weakness, then turn that into a goal of self-development, whether through learning or classes or courses.

- Use judgement to build emotional toughness – learn to stay calm and positive when facing judgement, this helps you be strong in handling future criticism better.

- Set growth goals – use self-judgement to set goals for personal development; let your reflections guide you.

- Check out your own biases – now we've reacted enough to others' judgement, it's time to reflect on how you judge others. *It's unfair to judge others first and foremost and keep complaining when others judge you, so first reflect and then react.*

You must have heard people saying, "Respond, *don't* react." But,

I would suggest "Reflect before you respond".

Let's talk about a few simple ways to use judgement for your personal growth, and it works like magic if you start doing it.

- Keep a growth log
- Set clear goals
- Learn from your mistakes
- Practice gratitude
- Surround yourself with positivity
- Reflect regularly
- Try to celebrate small wins
- Stay open-minded
- Develop a growth and progressive mindset

By integrating these practices, you can turn judgement into a powerful tool for growth and development.

Chapter 15

Judgement Unfolded:
Mr Bliss, Mr Blameworth,
and the Choice in Between

When my elder daughter stayed with her grandparents while I managed a busy career and daily chores in Mumbai, the whispers of judgement started creeping in.

- **Mr. Blameworth** was relentless: *"You're a bad mother. How could you leave your child behind? Other mothers balance it all, and you've failed at your most important duty."* His voice echoed in my mind, amplifying societal expectations and making me feel inadequate.

- **Mr. Bliss**, on the other hand, gently reminded me: *"Your daughter is in loving hands. She's getting attention, care, and bonding with her grandparents, which is priceless. You're building a foundation for her future."*

Caught between these voices, I had **The Choice in Between**. I could have let the judgement from others and my inner critic consume me, but instead, I chose to reflect on what truly mattered.

Later, when I saw how beautifully my daughter had developed under the care of her grandparents, I realised I'd been overgeneralising my fears. She thrived, and our bond only grew stronger. . **Mr. Bliss** was right all along: *"You were doing the best you could, and it all turned out okay. "*

Both Mr. Bliss and Mr. Blameworth represent different perspectives on judgement. From the lens of your cheerleader, Mr. Bliss, it will be positive and encouraging. From the lens of the critic, it will be negative and discouraging. Ultimately, this depends on your friends and the deep bond you share with them

Now, let's see how the same judgement can be handled differently by Mr. Bliss and Mr. Blameworth

1. "You could have done better in the presentation, Shalini."

    Mr. Bliss – I can learn from this and improve my presentation skills next time

    Mr Blameworth – Why am I not good enough? Why do I always mess up? and who is he to judge me or suggest me, I have seen his presentation skills also

2. Your project lacks creativity

    Mr Bliss – this is a chance to push myself and think outside the box

    Mr Blameworth – I am not creative enough to handle this, I will never get it right

3. Your project lacks creativity

    Mr Bliss – this is a chance to push myself and think outside the box

    Mr Blameworth – I am not creative enough to handle this, I will never get it right

4. You need to work on your communication skills

    Mr Bliss – I'll take this as an opportunity to work on my communication skills

    Mr Blameworth – I am terrible, and no one understands me, I should stop talking much

5. Your work is good but not exceptional.

    Mr Bliss – I will step up and deliver exceptional work next time; it's a challenge.

    Mr Blameworth – My work is never good enough, no matter how hard I try. I think I am in the wrong place; no one likes me.

6. You have made a lot of mistakes.

    Mr Bliss – Mistakes are part of learning, and I'll use this feedback to improve and will ensure I will not repeat these mistakes again.

    Mr Blameworth – I always mess things up, I am just not good enough

7. Your writing lacks emotion.

    Mr Bliss – Great feedback. Now let me work deeper to bring emotions into my book.

    Mr Blameworth – I am not a good writer, and I should stop writing.

8. You missed some really important details.

    Mr Bliss - I will be more careful next time and focus on my attention to detail.

    Mr Blameworth – I am always careless. I am not reliable enough.

Your cheerleader always pushes you to learn, grow, and improve, and the critic will always focus on limitations, self-doubt, and making judgements feel terrible.

It's your choice who you choose.

Chapter 16

Live Life With #Judgementfreecode and Create a Judgement Free Space

By now, you have understood what this fear of judgement looks like, where it comes from, and how it impacts us, along with powerful ways to gain freedom from this fear and live an authentic life.

I think it's time to create **judgement-free space**, which is a safe space or a sound environment where people feel safe to be themselves, free from fear of criticism and judgement.

Let's create not only a safe physical space but also a mental and emotional one filled with openness, understanding, and support.

Let's create a place of liberation, where freedom from societal norms and expectations is the primary goal, where you don't have to do something for others. In this space, you can express your ideas and emotions without even filtering them for the sake of others.

Why we need it

We live in a world where everyone is constantly evaluated — be it school, work, house, or on social media, and this constant assessment creates pressure to please others, which ultimately leads to stress, anxiety, or the fear of being judged.

When we have a judgement-free space, people can stop worrying about external validation and focus on their inner growth.

Let's make space around us where people are free to make mistakes, experiment, fall, learn, and express their emotions.

A judgement-free space is understanding that everyone is imperfect and vulnerable; it's about realising that we all have insecurities, fears, and doubts.

There is a growing focus on 'inclusivity,' with large organizations working towards this goal. There is a separate wing or department which is only working on inclusivity, which is good. ***We need to understand that creating a judgment-free space is deeply inclusive and fosters true acceptance.***

Let's set ourselves free and only focus on growth.

Judgement-free space is not just a safe space, whether it's in virtual or in the real world, but it's a ground of growth, creativity, and connections.

Let's create a judgement-free space around us with *#judgementfreecode*.

Last words before we meet again...

Now it's time to say goodbye, at least for now, before we meet again. But before you go, let me leave you with this.

Kudos to you for making it this far. If you have read this book and have decided to act, then you are already on the path to transform yourself - from someone bound by fear to an individual who is liberated from the judgement trap.

Today, everyone is talking about financial freedom, but what about **emotional freedom?**

When you achieve emotional freedom, then you release your pent-up emotions, work through your tough feelings and be honest about your struggles, because when you are not holding back or masking your true self, you experience emotional freedom and behave authentically **"Authenticity *is a superpower"*** and only superheroes can truly embrace it.

I wish you all the best as you gain this superpower and become your most authentic self, ready to live an empowered and true life.

Here is a simple trick to kick-start this journey. Go on a full day without judging anyone or anything around you, no judgement about people, situations, or even posts on social media. Why? Because this makes you truly cool.

While we can't change the world or the judgments around us, we can become wise in how we judge. Remember, "judgment is a thoughtful process, and it requires a healthy mind"

Remember, being non-judgemental is the new cool. So, let's live by a new code - ***#judgementfreecode***

See you soon with another life-transforming topic, till then, **Be authentic, be a hero**.

Bio

Shalini is an alumna of the prestigious IIM Kozhikode and IIM Jammu, holding multiple management degrees. She currently works in a global role at one of the top 10 organisations in the world. Hailing from Nalanda, Bihar, the birthplace of the world's first residential international university, Shalini's journey is a testament to the power of determination and dreams.

Now settled in Mumbai with her husband and two children, she balances a fulfilling family life with a successful professional career and a strong commitment to societal contribution.

Her incredible journey from rural India to a prominent corporate position has been driven by a relentless passion for self-improvement and a strong desire to help others. In her debut book, *The Judgement Trap*, Shalini not only shares her personal journey but also provides actionable strategies to overcome fear and judgement, realising one's true potential. Her story proves that passion can conquer and encourages readers to pursue their dreams and become the most authentic version of themselves.

"Stay connected! Follow Shalini on Instagram @shalini.k.vardhan, visit www.shalinivardhan.com or reach out via email at Shalini.kumari0704@gmail.com for more inspiration and updates"

Synopsis

The Judgement trap reveals how the fear of judgement can restrain potential and hinder personal growth. Drawing from the authors' inspiring journey — from a village in Nalanda, Bihar to thriving in a global role in one of the fortune 500 organisations in the world.

This book resonates with young adults and professionals who grapple with self-doubt and societal expectations.

Through relatable stories and practical insights, the author explores how the pressure to fit in can lead to missed opportunities, distorted dreams, and an unfulfilling life.

This book talks about the root cause of this fear and how it's been ingrained in a person from oneself, family, or the surroundings, its dissection, and how this is impacting our life.

The book also introduces multiple approaches which work like a transformative framework designed to help readers challenge their inner voice and embrace authenticity.

The book also introduces 2 characters, Mr Bliss and Mr Blameworth, within us, where one works like a cheerleader and the other like a critic. Your connection with them defines how we see judgement around us and how you can use judgement as a growth tool with the help of Mr.Bliss.

Each chapter guides readers through actionable strategies to build confidence, celebrate small wins with the growth mindset, and cultivate a safe and judgement-free community.

This book will offer you scientifically proven techniques to:

- Break free from fear

- Build genuine confidence

- Embrace your true self and live fearlessly and authentically

- Master 11 actionable techniques to manage self-doubt, navigate social situations confidently, and silence your inner critic for greater peace of mind

- Experience real happiness and personal growth

By the end of the book, readers will be empowered to rise above fear and judgement, unlocking their true selves and achieving their aspirations.

The judgement trap is not just a call to action, it's a heartfelt invitation to live boldly, dream fearlessly and step into one's full potential. So, are you ready to break free?